Anthra by
Charles Edgar Patience

Juanita Patience Moss

WILLOW BEND BOOKS
2006

WILLOW BEND BOOKS
AN IMPRINT OF HERITAGE BOOKS, INC.

Books, CDs, and more—Worldwide

For our listing of thousands of titles see our website
at
www.HeritageBooks.com

Published 2006 by
HERITAGE BOOKS, INC.
Publishing Division
65 East Main Street
Westminster, Maryland 21157-5026

Other books by the author:

Battle of Plymouth, North Carolina (April 17-20, 1864): The Last Confederate Victory
Created to Be Free: A Historical Novel about One American Family
The Forgotten Black Soldiers in White Regiments During the Civil War

Cover: C. Edgar Patience engraving front of King's College altar
Wilkes-Barre, Pennsylvania, 1956 (courtesy of *Ebony* magazine)

International Standard Book Number: 0-7884-4263-5

This book is dedicated to my husband
of fifty-four years

EDWARD IRVING MOSS

He may not be a PATIENCE, but his infinite <u>patience</u>
has allowed me to spend countless hours at my
computer after I unexpectedly became an author.

"No medium lends itself more to the creating of the simplified form of abstract art than does anthracite coal. Its rich velvety blackness when polished to perfection makes each sculptured piece unique and a delight to the eye."

Charles Edgar Patience
(1906-1972)

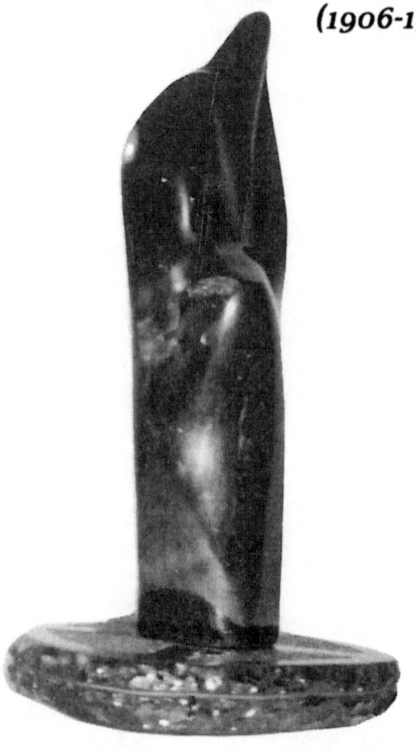

Fig. 1. "Dolphin" (property of author)

TABLE OF CONTENTS

Genealogy

Ancestors of Charles Edgar Patience

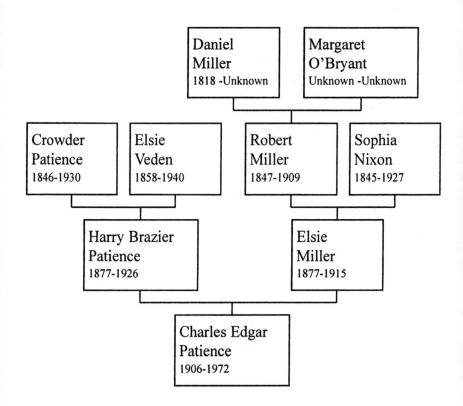

Acknowledgements

My gratitude is extended to each person who contributed to this book in any manner, beginning with African and African American art appraiser Alvah Taylor Beander. For several years since I began writing my books, she has been encouraging me to document my father's unique work. Also, Chester Kulesa, the Historic Site Administrator at the Anthracite Heritage Museum in Scranton, Pennsylvania, has alerted me to the fact that students researching Charles Edgar Patience's anthracite art are unable to find very much information. Therefore, I have written this book about this unique African American sculptor whose work is known in northeastern Pennsylvania, but not in other locales.

Family members encouraging me in this venture include my first cousins Betty Patience Claiborne, daughter of Wilmer Miller Patience and collector of her Uncle Edgar's works, and Katherine Patience Kennedy, whose father Kenneth Veden Patience also had carved coal art, but did not make it his life's work. For inclusion in this book Katherine has photographed several pieces of her father's work that is prominently displayed in her Bronx, New York, home.

In addition, Dorothy Walker Smith, a close family friend and owner of a piece of C. Edgar Patience's anthracite sculpture, had her's photographed by Jim Collier. She also provided the names of two other collectors, Sondra Meyers and Myer Alprin of Scranton who granted permission for Warren Rowe to photograph sculptures displayed in their individual homes.

Linda Paul photographed the anthracite altar in the King's College Chapel, as well as the sculpture that is the property of Blue Cross of Northeastern Pennsylvania, both in Wilkes-Barre. Reba Burruss-Barnes, my publicist, accompanied me to Scranton and to Lewisburg, Pennsylvania, as well as to the Smithsonian Storage Facility in Suitland, Maryland, where she photographed as I researched. Due to the high polish, anthracite art is very reflective and therefore, a challenge to photograph.

Ruth Helgemo was my guide when viewing the anthracite altar in the beautiful Chancel of St. Peter's Lutheran Church in Hanover Township and provided me with pertinent information concerning it. My cousin LeRoy Patience accompanied me to photograph the altar. John W. Franklin, Program Manager of the Center for Folklife and Cultural Heritage at the Smithsonian Institution, escorted me to the storage facility where, hidden from public view, is an anthracite monolith that had been shaped and polished by my father in 1961. Throughout the past forty-five years, I have been asked about its whereabouts at the Smithsonian Institution, and finally in 2004, I was successful in discovering the answer. Later I was able to obtain the necessary permission for viewing and photographing it.

Frank Magdalinski, one of the few remaining Wyoming Valley coal carvers, has created a special process for preventing anthracite art from deterioration since it does not have the durability of harder materials such as marble. He has played an important role in the preservation of the altar created by my father for King's College.

My friend and colleague, Dr. June Bohannon Powell, retired Department Chairperson of Language Arts at Bloomfield High School, Bloomfield, New Jersey, has edited this book as she did each my other books. Rosette Graham, Layout and Graphics Coordinator, has lent her expertise in formatting the manuscript.

Dr. Catherine Hastings, professor of English at Susquehanna University, researched the genealogy of the Miller family of Hartley Township, Pennsylvania. Carolyn Crowe, president of the African American Historical and Genealogical Society (AAHGS), created an ancestral chart for Charles Edgar Patience. Carolyn DuBose, writer of the 1970 *EBONY* magazine article, contributed a photograph of herself while interviewing my father, as well as a copy of his "Thank you" letter.

Dr. Margaret Corgan, Chairperson of the Department of Foreign Languages and Literatures at King's College, provided additional article and other information concerning the anthracite coal altar donated by her family to King's College. High school classmates Nancy Ardoline and Roy Kylander pleasantly surprised me with the photographs they mailed.

Recently, Betty Patience Claiborne donated her extensive coal art collection to the Anthracite Heritage Museum in Scranton, Pennsylvania. This indeed, is a valuable gift to posterity because that museum provided the environment necessary for preserving and displaying the anthracite coal art of C. Edgar Patience.

The 100th birth-date of Charles Edgar Patience is 27 August 1906. Therefore, I think it quite appropriate that the Betty Patience Claiborne Collection be opened to the public on the day of her birthday, 26 August 2006, as a means of saying "Thank you" for her generosity. The Collection is joining four major works of C. Edgar Patience already on display at the Museum.

—Juanita Patience Moss

A Short Testimony on the

Anthracite Coal Sculptor

Charles Edgar Patience

Through the medium of anthracite or hard coal, a fossil fuel, C. Edgar Patience created a kind of sculpture that helps to preserve the dignity of a time in northeastern Pennsylvania when "anthracite was king." The coal-industry helped fuel America's industrial revolution and "anthracite people" formed a unique culture area.

Mr. Patience believed that the beauty of anthracite could be revealed best through sculpture. The selection of coal with a dense, hard composition was essential to compliment the quality of his artistic skills and talent. Mr. Patience's anthracite sculptures display an appreciation of history combined with a keen awareness of his place in the twentieth century. His hard coal works range from expressions of matters close to his heart, such as his family and African-American culture, to large commissioned pieces including corporate trademarks and historical subjects.

The legacy of C. Edgar Patience's art and life is part of the heritage of the anthracite region of northeastern Pennsylvania. His sculptures are an important link to the past for all of us to enjoy and learn from. His life, as a man of conscience and purpose, serves as a role model for future generations and is an inspiration to us all.

Chester J. Kulesa, Historic Site Administrator
Pennsylvania Anthracite Heritage Museum
Scranton, Pennsylvania

Fig. 2. *Portrait of C. Edgar Patience above his anthracite bust of George Washington at the Anthracite Heritage Museum, Scranton, Pa.*

Introduction
by
Alvah Taylor Beander

THE LEGACY OF PATIENCE

While having a casual conversation with Juanita Patience Moss one afternoon, she mentioned that her father had been an artist. Keenly interested, I asked, "What's his name?"

When she answered, "Edgar Patience," I hesitated to mention that as an appraiser of African and African American Art, I wasn't familiar with him and his work. I was not embarrassed or bothered that I did not know who he was, though, because there have been many African American artists in the 1940s who were critically acclaimed artists, but there was scant academic documentation and an erratic market presence. They all suffered from a weak and volatile infrastructure. Galleries and museum representation and exhibitions of African American artists were limited. Most African American artists were not part of a movement or group that garnered media attention or benefactors. They were largely overlooked and underrepresented.

As Juanita continued with her father's history, I began to think of my resources and references so that I could begin my search. After all, my strength was in my research. Before going too far with my thoughts, Juanita brought me back to the present. She was mentioning that her father worked in an unusual medium—coal.

"Coal? Did she say coal?"

I know that I had never seen or read anything about an African American sculptor of coal. For the record, I also thought to myself, "Isn't coal a black substance that is found in the mining of energy resources underground that is dirty and toxic? Why would he pick coal to create sculptures?"

A better question to ask, of course, is why not work with coal since it was a major part of his everyday environment? Coal was a natural resource that was organic, plentiful, and easy to carve (Moh's scale 2.5-3). The Wyoming Valley offered an abundance of

"Pennsylvania black diamonds" for the craftsmen. The legacy of fine wood carvers also extends from the African continent of our forbearers. Edgar may not have consciously been aware perhaps of his atavistic memory when he chose to sculpt beautiful utilitarian objects of art.

Juanita, being the wonderful storyteller that she is, painted a picture of her grandfather starting a commercial coal business of jewelry and artifacts. Juanita's grandfather passed the skill and technique to his six sons, but it was "C. Edgar Patience," who would continue the legacy.

Juanita's father received public recognition as he presented his art to international and domestic dignitaries; exhibiting at the 1939 World's Fair; while also shaping and polishing the massive chunk of coal intended for the Mining and Minerals Industries Hall of Coal at the Smithsonian Institution. He used those opportunities and others while honing the fine business acumen it took to run a business full time while creating art.

THE PATIENCE OF THE PATIENCE

Today, we talk a lot about our purpose, our authentic selves, and life's journeys. We look inside and try to understand our purpose and to share it with others. The beauty of finding our purpose in life is that the universe generally supports its correctness and offers us a platform for growth. Purpose, while formed within, flourishes when nurtured in our families and communities. Edgar was certainly supported by his father and you will see that the small Pennsylvania town of West Pittston supported him, as well.

Interestingly, the foundation for the pivotal transitional period in the business was the desire in their hearts to design something that was favored by both men. The heart, representing the symbolic love between the father and his sons, became their signature. The beat of the heart is also considered the rhythmic foundation of the African drum that clearly represents the atavistic memories.

Years passed and I constantly reminded Juanita of the importance of introducing us to the rest of her family. She had written about her great grandfather and stepmother. I hoped that the time would come when she would introduce her father. Her straightforward delivery of the narrative teaches the reader that artistic expression can be represented in many ways through the life experiences and the limited resources in any regional culture. The research process was difficult, but Juanita was patient.

Edgar put his heart into his art. I can only imagine the excitement and honor he must have felt to have his first television interview. Unfortunately, it was after this wonderful accomplishment that Edgar became ill from "miner's asthma," a condition he developed from working with coal. Ironically, the material necessary to create his art was now the cause of his life to end.

Napoleon Hill, author of the timeless *Think and Grow Rich*, was quoted as saying: *"Patience, persistence, and perspiration make an unbeatable combination for success."*

For Edgar Patience, patience, persistence, perspiration, and a signature heart were successful. Without a doubt, his father would have been proud of Edgar's accomplishments; for he had trusted his son's vision, talent, and skills.

**Fig. 3.** *C. Edgar Patience carving "George Washington" circa 1945*

Photographs

__Fig. 4.__ Lettering begun and polished lettering completed

Fig. 5. *WEST PITTSTON HIGH SCHOOL 1924 YEARBOOK*

EDGAR PATIENCE
(Sic 'em)

Edgar showed his real ability in the capacity of stage manager at our Senior play. On the cinders he's surely a fast boy.

"Fresh and strong the world we seize, world of labor and of ease."

Football (3), (4); Baseball (3), (4); Track (Mgr.) (4); Bazaar; Comet; Class Day.

Prologue

Like most fathers, mine, when I was a child, would set out early in the day for his place of employment. First though, he had to consume his bowlful of steaming oatmeal with the requisite dollop of butter, two heaping teaspoons of sugar, and a splash of the rich pure cream that had risen to the top of the glass bottle left on the front porch by the milkman before dawn.

Then he was off to work. Exiting the kitchen onto the latticed back porch, he would step into coveralls similar to those worn by coal miners over trousers and dingy once-white undershirts. After donning his work cap, he descended the wooden steps from the porch to the narrow path leading through the backyard that faced one of the alleys so common to many Pennsylvania towns.

Originally, the alleys had been designed for the horses, wagons, and carriages traversing to and from stables set behind residences and businesses. Differing from some Pennsylvania communities like Dillsburg where my father's paternal grandmother had spent her childhood, the alleys of West Pittston are named.

Unlike most fathers, though, my father's place of employment was not at some distant location. Rather, his was the small rectangular wooden building at the rear of our backyard. Always referred to as "The Shop," its windowed western side faced the alley to benefit from the stronger afternoon light.

My father's father had built "The Shop" during the early 20th century for his growing coal carving business. A small antechamber served as an office where a telephone had been wired. In wintertime that narrow front room was kept comfortably warm by a small coal-burning pot-bellied iron stove. The larger room, on the other hand, was not heated and subsequently, could become quite chilly. That back room was filled with all kinds of machinery essential to the coal carving business, some having been built by the original carver himself.

As a child I would never venture into "The Shop" much farther than the antechamber. Whenever I needed to talk with my father about something really important, I would just open the door to the extremely dusty "inner sanctum" and shout at the top of my voice, "Daddy!" – sometimes being forced to do so several times before he would hear me over the din of the clattering machinery. Since I do not remember ever going very far into that room, I cannot describe it in any great detail.

All I can remember is that it was very noisy and extremely dirty—no place I had any desire to be. I, personally, did not like being dirty, and that is my response whenever asked if I ever had an interest in the coal carving business. My father seemed not to mind the dirt because his clothing was always covered with coal dust from his cap to his shoes until he would remove them on the back porch of 34 Washington Street in the small borough of West Pittston located in northeastern Pennsylvania.

Even though never having worked in "The Shop," as a teenager I did make contributions to the business. Opportunities came whenever my father or his youngest brother Harold carried into the kitchen pantry flat wooden boxes filled with highly polished ashtrays and paperweights, as well as thermometer and pincushion holders.

For each item I washed in warm soapy water, rinsed, and dried, I would receive a whole nickel. That really seemed like a lot of money to this girl in the mid 1940s. In addition, I enjoyed creating vivid colored satin "pumpkins" for stuffing into gleaming anthracite pincushion holders. A dime was earned for each of those.

From the first grade to graduate school, whenever an opportunity would present itself, I shared my father's unique art with intrigued classmates and instructors to earn an "A." Now I am pleased once again to be sharing it with you, my readers.

Much of the information in this book has been compiled from numerous newspaper clippings and magazine articles written throughout the years about the work of my father, Charles Edgar Patience (always addressed by his middle name). After the death of my stepmother, Alice Patterson Patience, I discovered in 2001 the clippings and articles she had stored away in boxes. She had intended to organize them some day, but, unfortunately, she became blind before getting around to doing so. Consequently, I do not know the sources of a number of the newspaper clippings, but I have cited those I do know while attempting to correct some misinformation persisting even today.

Hopefully, students and any other persons interested in the unusual art of Charles Edgar Patience will find this book valuable. In order that the original documents are taken care of properly for future generations, I have donated them to the Moorland-Springarn Research Center at Howard University, Washington, D.C., where they may be viewed by appointment. Similar information also has been sent to the Library of Congress, the Smithsonian Institution, and the Schomburg Center for Research in Black Culture in New York City.

Fig. 6. Charles Edgar Patience at age twenty-six in 1932
(photo by Howard Reid)

***Fig. 7**. The anthracite coal sculptor C. Edgar Patience in his work clothes*
circa 1950

CHAPTER 1
What Is Coal?

I always have taken a great deal of pleasure in wearing the beautiful anthracite coal jewelry created by my father, Charles Edgar Patience. Oftentimes I will ask people what they think the black stone might be, should they admire my jewelry. Most of the time I am answered incorrectly with, "*Onyx*," which is exactly what I expect to hear. To my delighted surprise, however, every once in a while someone will recognize it as coal.

More than likely, though, I first must offer the hint, "*I'm from Pennsylvania.*" Then someone may venture to guess, "*Coal?*" in a very dubious tone.

"*Yes, it is coal,*" I will answer. "*You are absolutely correct.*"

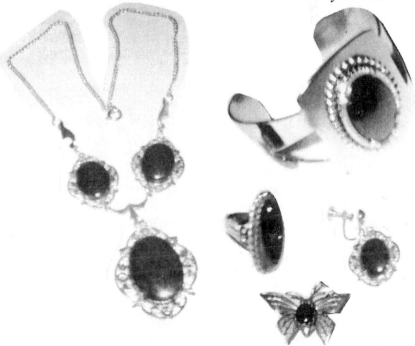

Fig. 8. *Anthracite necklace, earring, bracelet, ring, and pin created for Alice Patterson Patience (property of author)*

Depending upon the age, locale, and life experiences of the persons I may be querying, the word "coal" can elicit various responses. For instance, many young people will immediately think of the charcoal they use for their outdoor grills. However, most persons over fifty years of age born in northeastern Pennsylvania will know exactly what coal is.

In all probability, due to memories of its burning in iron kitchen, living room, and dining room pot-bellied stoves or in cellar furnaces (should their families have been more prosperous than many), those persons will describe coal as being black and very dirty. They easily will remember the local coal man whose truck delivered a ton or two or five, depending upon family finances, to pour noisily down steel chutes through open cellar windows into empty coal bins. They will recall that much simpler time when neighborhood kids could find excitement just in congregating in someone's yard to watch the familiar sight. Certainly, too, they will remember the heavy wooden-handled iron coal shovels, tin coal-pails with smaller shovels, and piles and piles of ashes that resulted from the burning of coal.

Unfortunately, there were people who could not afford the coal man's delivery and so were forced daily to crawl the sides of mountainous culm banks [1] to pick their own coal from the debris that had been brought up from the mines. Mostly women and children, toting brown burlap bags over their shoulders or buckets in their hands, all the while praying to be able to find enough to warm their frigid shanties and to cook their evening meals.

Some of those same persons over fifty years of age who were born in northeastern Pennsylvania will know without a doubt what coal is, because family members and friends had labored in the mines where many died tragically from accidents due to cave-ins of falling rocks or suffocation by noxious gases. Or they might have died years later from the ravages of anthracosis or "black lung disease" due to inhaling fine particles of coal dust for years. [2]

♦♦♦

Throughout the years, many people had asked the same question, *"Just what is coal?"* For instance, in Wilkes-Barre, Pennsylvania, Judge Jesse Fell was one of the quizzical when he had stated in 1829, the year before his death, *"When, how or of what matter it was formed I do not know and do not ever expect to know, but its usefulness we do know and appreciate, still believing its use to be as yet only in its infancy."* [3]

Judge Fell was a popular innkeeper in need of keeping the rooms of his establishment warm and comfortable for his customers, mainly local men who enjoyed gathering there in the evenings. Because the nearby woods were disappearing rapidly due to farmers clearing the land, an alternative source of fuel very much was needed.

Blacksmiths for years had been using the shiny black rock found in outcrops scattered all over Wyoming Valley. The brothers Obadiah and Daniel Gore, for instance, had burned the black rock for their prosperous smithing business back in 1769. Thirty-seven years later Judge Fell pondered over the possibility of using it in his barroom fireplace since all the tools he would need were a pick and a shovel.

Even though Judge Fell knew the black rock to be combustible, he also knew that it would require a steady supply of air. Blacksmiths used bellows, impractical, though, for the Judge's establishment. So on 11 February 1808, he made an attempt to find a method for burning the black rock efficiently. Consequently, due to the success of one simple experiment in his Wilkes-Barre tavern at the corner of South Washington and Northampton Streets, the anthracite coal mining industry was launched in northeastern Pennsylvania. [4]

Judge Jesse Fell recorded in his journal, *"[I] made the experiment of burning the common stone coal of the valley in a grate, in a common fireplace in my house, and find it will answer the purpose of fuel, making a clearer and better fire, at less expense, than burning wood in the common way."* [5]

Most likely, Judge Fell never learned what coal actually is. He probably never knew that it is a fossil fuel formed from terrestrial plants during the Carboniferous Era.[6] Coal is combustible sedimentary rock. Under extreme pressure and high temperatures through eons of years, huge accumulations of vegetable matter such as extinct tree ferns had been changed both physically and chemically.

As a result, in various places of the world differing carbonaceous forms developed, metamorphosing first from peat to lignite, then to coal, and lastly to diamonds. The hardest coal, anthracite, has been dubbed "black diamond," since diamonds are the final stage of the carbon creations and consequently, the hardest.

The term "hardness," measured in Moh's Scale, refers to a mineral's resistance to abrasion. A mineral is identified numerically from 1 (softest-talc) to 10 (hardest-diamond). The anthracite coal, found only in northeastern Pennsylvania, has a hardness of 2.5 to 3 in Moh's Scale. [7] Very easily scratched, it is quite amenable to carving.

Fig. 9. *"Coal-Miner"*

CHAPTER 2
World Wide Use of Coal

Coal has been found in nearly every part of the world, nowhere, though, in quantities as great as those in the United States and to the surprise of many, even in Alaska where the one remaining operating mine is located near Fairbanks. Being much younger than the coal found in the "lower 49," Alaskan coal is softer. [8]

Exactly when the initial use of coal as a fuel began is not known. Even though people had been familiar with its combustible qualities for several thousands of years, not until the 18th and 19th centuries would it become an indispensable source of energy.

The earliest reference to coal can be found in the writings of Aristotle and his pupil Theoprastus, who mentioned a coal-like substance existing in Thrace and northwestern Italy. Another later reference mentioned the use of coal by occupying Romans in Britain before the year 400 A. D. However, its use must not have been universal among them, since the coal outcrops in conquered France were ignored when Roman aqueducts were built there. [9]

The *Domesday Book* in 1085 listed everything of economic value in England at that time. Until 1200, no mention was made of the mining of coal. Other than the early use of coal by the Romans, no other reference has been found regarding coal mining in Great Britain. The earliest known recorded commercial use of coal was for the smelting of copper in Asia at the Fu-Shun mine in Manchuria between 1290 and 1300. [10]

In the United States coal was discovered first in 1673 by Louis Joliet and Father Jacques Marquette in Illinois and later in 1680 by Rene-Robert La Salle. Soon afterwards in 1701, coal was found in Virginia's Richmond Basin where possibly the coal mining industry in the New World may have begun, [11] paralleling the mining practices of Great Britain, especially Wales from which many experienced miners were induced to emigrate. [12]

Found in veins (seams) sometimes as thick as twenty-seven feet, anthracite and bituminous are the main types of coal found in the United States. However, only in northeastern Pennsylvania between the Delaware and Susquehanna Rivers did the low sulfur, relatively clean burning hard anthracite develop. [13] Due to the coal's being lodged in highly compressed earth, much of the sulfur [14] was squeezed from the anthracite. Characterized by its brilliant blackness and conchoidal fracture (break), [15] anthracite became a desirable domestic fuel, capable of burning much longer and with much less smoke than other kinds of coal.

Bituminous, the high sulfur softer coal used in industry, is mined in great abundance in western Pennsylvania, as well as in other states, such as Alabama, Illinois, Kentucky, Ohio, and West Virginia. Contrasted with the conchoidal fracture of the much harder anthracite, most bituminous coals have a regular fracture. [16]

Since bituminous coal is softer, jewelry made from it is less durable than that made from anthracite and, therefore, needs the protection of a special finish. [17] In contrast, the harder and naturally brilliant anthracite is excellent for carving and requires no application of a finish.

Fig. 10. Anthracite Clock

Northeastern Pennsylvania once had been an exceptionally beautiful verdant region characterized by tall grasses and thick forests of mixed evergreen and deciduous trees. Mantled in deep green during summer, the mountain ranges colored brilliantly in autumn.

Flowing south from upper New York State to the Chesapeake Bay, the Susquehanna River had cut through the Appalachian Mountains eons ago forming the twenty-three mile long Wyoming Valley. Once the crystal clear Susquehanna had abounded with several species of edible fish and for centuries Native Americans, such as the Nanticokes, fished by the banks of the river.

During the 17th century, however, William Penn followers ("Pennamites") displaced the Native Americans. Then sometime later, "Yankees" from Connecticut arrived to mine the rich iron ore fields in the northern region, causing a conflict between the two factions of Englishmen. Consequently, before the "Pennamites" could lay total claim to the land, a series of Yankee-Pennamite Wars were fought. [18]

During the 19th century, anthracite coal would become "king" after its discovery in Nesquehoning (Native American for "narrow valley"). However, while putting Wyoming Valley "on the map," "Coal-Barons" claiming the land destroyed much of the valley's natural beauty by building large collieries [19] with rumbling rearing coal breakers [20] and overcrowded "company patches." [21]

Like phoenixes rising from the ashes, ugly dark mountainous culm piles rose from the mines to disrupt the horizon. Further spoiling the original beauty of the Valley, railroads and canals cut swathes through the land for the coal to be transported.

Fig. 11. "Forest Scene" etching (property of the author)

Fig. 12. *A typical coal colliery*
(courtesy of the Anthracite Heritage Museum)

To protect millions of Americans against winter weather, the thriving coal mining industry would employ thousands of European immigrants, among them English, Germans, Irish, Italians, Lithuanians, Polish, Russians, Slovaks, and Welsh. [22] Many boys, some as young as eight years of age, were hired as "breaker boys."

In addition to the European immigrants, at the end of the 19th century black men also searching for employment opportunities flocked to Wyoming Valley to work at the coal collieries. Over the ensuing years a number of "Coal-Barons" were to make their fortunes, sadly, however, at the expense of countless poor men and boys who would die from accidents at the mines or from the lingering effects of respiratory diseases.

Fig. 13. Breaker boys toiling at a colliery
(courtesy of the Anthracite Heritage Museum)

Fig. 14. **Breaker boys circa 1900**
(courtesy of Anthracite Heritage Museum)

CHAPTER 3
Pennsylvania Coal Carvers

Even though during the 17th and 18th centuries, the art form of coal carving had been popular in northern England, interest in it gradually died. Perhaps one reason was that the type of coal found there easily fractured, thereby requiring a special type of skill and patience. More recently, an inventive 20th century coal carver named Ernest Holder of Portslade in Sussex, England, covered his intricate jet [23] carvings with emery dust to produce a smooth porcelain-like finish. [24]

Being from a family of two generations of coal carvers, my father was aware that carving coal for a livelihood in northeastern Pennsylvania was becoming a dying art. He explained, "*When I was a child, every boy who handled coal carved it. I can name a dozen men who still do it for a hobby. But most of them don't stick to it.*" [25]

Ironically, just as Charles Edgar Patience was reaching the pinnacle of his career, anthracite coal mining was going downhill and quality anthracite was becoming extremely difficult to locate, especially for his more ambitious projects. Also, just as his talent finally was becoming recognized and appreciated, he contracted second-degree form of "miner's asthma," a disease he referred to as an occupational hazard and which ultimately caused his death in 1972. Attired in work clothes always covered with fine particles of coal dust, he worked in a small, insufficiently ventilated basement shop crammed with drills, lathes, wheels, and other necessary tools. On his workbench lay a surgical mask for protecting his mouth and nose, but he readily admitted he was inconsistent about wearing it. [26]

◆◆◆

Another man who had stuck to coal carving for his livelihood was Charles Cunningham from Summit Hill, Pennsylvania. He died in 1971 at the age of eighty-two. Having learned his skills from his father, James Cunningham, Charles began carving in 1901, beginning his apprenticeship at the age of twelve.

One of his best works was a three-foot long, sixty-pound replica of a steam locomotive and tender, permanently on display at the Anthracite Heritage Museum in Scranton, Pennsylvania. It was first exhibited at the 1939 World's Fair in New York City. [27]

Another of his works is the "Hunk of Coal" Trophy, an exact replica of a football, commissioned in 1952 by the B-M 25 Club. The agreement was that the trophy would be retained by the winner of the annual Thanksgiving game between rivals Bloomfield and Montclair High Schools in northern New Jersey. [28]

When I began teaching at Bloomfield High School in 1958, I was quite surprised to see the anthracite trophy. My colleagues thought it was my father's work. However, I knew immediately that it was not since usually I am able to recognize his style.

I was aware of the trophy being exchanged for a number of years until the practice was discontinued. Today the Cunningham football trophy is housed permanently at Montclair High School, interestingly, my children's Alma Mater. [29]

◆◆◆

Presently working in Plains Township, Pennsylvania, are two other members of the dying breed of anthracite coal sculptors. They are the brothers Anthony, Jr. and Frank Magdalinski who also learned coal-carving techniques from their father. Anthony, Sr., however, was forced to retire in the late 1950s due to a work related accident that disabled one of his hands. In addition, he suffered from third-degree "miner's asthma" due to inhaling coal dust for decades.

After graduating from college in 1966, Frank chose to continue his father's trade and two years later he and his brother Anthony started their own small company, "Anthracite Coal Crafts." [30] One major difference between the techniques of the father and his sons is that Anthony Magdalinski, Sr. always had used a lumber saw to cut his large pieces of coal, but Frank today uses a much more efficient twenty-inch silicon-carbon blade made in Chicago.

No longer able to obtain a satisfactory supply of quality hard coal, Frank has created a coal dust resin mixture that can be called "composite coal." With this mixture, mine-related items such as donkeys, miners, and even jewelry that otherwise would be very expensive to manufacture can be produced economically.

During the past forty years, the demand for anthracite coal has dwindled drastically in industry, as well as for residence and business heating. Consequently, due to a lack of suitable supplies, with coal dust being so dangerous to respiratory health, and because of the necessary long and tedious hours of labor, the craft is not attracting many 21st century carvers.

In the words of Frank Magdalinski, who as a young man more than thirty years ago, had admired the work of Charles Edgar Patience when he exhibited at the annual Fine Arts Fiesta on the Wilkes-Barre Public Square, *"When you consider all of the above factors, you can see why it is getting difficult to acquire good quality anthracite coal to do sculpting. It is becoming a dying art and I am sad to say that within the next fifteen years, it will probably be a lost one."*[31]

***Fig. 15.** Trophy carved by Frank Magdalinski presented to author's sister-in-law, Constance Wynn (photo by Joseph Milcavage 2006)*

Fig. 16. C. Edgar Patience exhibiting at the Fine Arts Fiesta on Public Square, Wilkes-Barre, Pa. (photo by Gawlas 1969)

CHAPTER 4
Patience Family Carvers

The anthracite coal carving business associated with the Patiences began at the family home in Sturmersville, Pennsylvania. Later called Exeter Township, that particular area eventually became the northwest tip of the borough of West Pittston.

Interestingly, the business actually began as a hobby. When my grandfather, Harry Brazier Patience, was a boy during the latter part of the 19th century, whittling wood was a popular pastime for American males. Every boy carried a penknife in his pocket. However, instead of using wood, Harry whittled objects from chunks of shiny black anthracite coal.

The first son of Crowder and Elsie Veden Patience, Harry was the second of eight children. His father had been an eighteen-year old runaway slave who gained his freedom by joining the 103rd Pennsylvania Volunteer Infantry Regiment on 1 January 1864 when it was garrisoned at Plymouth, North Carolina. After the Civil War had ended, Crowder, having no intentions of ever returning to North Carolina, remained in Pennsylvania, later migrating east to the Wyoming Valley from Harrisburg where he had been mustered out of the Union Army on 13 July 1865. [32]

After settling his family in 1877 in the northeastern part of the state, for over forty years he would be employed by the prosperous owners of the Carpenter Greenhouses as a teamster and a farmer. [33] Comfortable living accommodations were provided by the Carpenters for Crowder and his family, continuing even after his death in 1930 and until his wife passed away ten years later. The Patiences were among the first of several African American families employed in West Pittston, Pennsylvania, at the end of the 19th century. [34]

After completing the eighth grade in the West Pittston Public Schools, fourteen-year old Harry found employment as a breaker boy at the Exeter Colliery, just as did many other young boys in town. However, at age seventeen after injuring his arm in a conveyor, [35] he left the coal mining business to start a small business of his own.

When Harry first began carving coal, his primitive equipment had consisted merely of a penknife and a wooden board covered by a tightly stretched piece of coverall material. His technique was to rub chalk on the cloth first and then to polish his completed work to a high semi-metallic gleam. [36]

Following his marriage to Elsie Miller, daughter of Robert and Sophia Nixon Miller of Hartley Township, Pennsylvania, [37] Harry moved his growing business from his parents' home at 828 Luzerne Avenue to his own at 16 Bond Street. [38] In his backyard he built a small shop with electrical equipment for cutting and shaping chunks of coal and for polishing his finished products with jeweler's compounds.

HARRY B. PATIENCE

MANUFACTURER OF

COAL NOVELTIES

OF EVERY DESCRIPTION

16 Bond Street

Fig. 17. Letterhead for 16 Bond Street, West Pittston, Pa. circa 1910

Fig. 18. Elsie Miller Patience, wife of Harry B. Patience circa 1900
(1877-1913)

Fig. 19. Harry Brazier Patience circa 1910
(1877-1926)

C. Edgar Patience explained once to a reporter how his father had begun carving coal when he was a breaker boy (slate picker). *"Breaker boys were eight to fifteen year olds who picked slate and rock from the freshly mined coal before it went into breakers for crunching into domestic sizes. The breaker boys were always keeping an eye out for unusually attractive pieces of coal, and when they found some they'd try to carve art objects. My father was quite adept at it, and made little things he sold to friends for a few pennies each. He did so well that eventually he established his own little business."* [39]

Fig. 20. Breaker boys at the Exeter Colliery circa 1899
Harry's younger brother Percy sits on left

Harry's business grew rapidly with his most popular items being highly polished hearts of differing sizes. Some were plain while others were designed with a circle of sulfur pyrite ("Pennsylvania diamonds") in the center. [40] Some had a number of smaller sparkling circles of pyrite placed evenly around the edges. On still others he carved small leaves to decorate both sides of the sparkling pyrite center, thereby adding what might be called the "Patience signature."

Recently, a close family friend showed me a coal heart she had spied and purchased at a yard sale in New Jersey. [41] Being the only person there who knew what the black stone was, she was curious to learn if it were my father's work and was anxious for my opinion. Once my eyes landed on the four small leaves etched on the heart, I knew it was Patience work. However, I cannot say with certainly which "Patience" the carver was. My grandfather, Harry B. Patience, had originated the "signature," but all of his sons had carved hearts, as well.

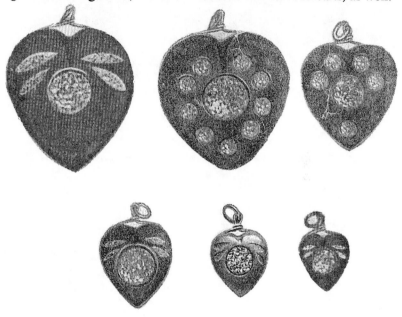

Fig. 21. Various styles of hearts carved by Harry B. Patience's Sons circa 1920

Fig. 22. Miscellaneous charms

Fig. 23. Harry B. Patience's Sons
Front: Edgar, Robert, Harry B.
Standing: Percy, Kenneth, Wilmer, Bruce
(circa 1918)

Fig. 24. Youngest son Harold when too young to work in "The Shop"
circa 1918

Fig. 25. 34 Washington St., West Pittston, Pa. circa 1920
Fig. 26. Harry B. Patience's Sons business card

After Harry's sudden demise in 1926 at age forty-eight due to a stroke, his married older sons attempted to continue their father's business. However, it was not lucrative enough to collectively support their families, and so they sought employment elsewhere. For instance, the eldest son Robert moved to Philadelphia. The second son Kenneth set out on his own and for a number of years maintained small coal carving shops, first in Wilkes-Barre and then in Harding where he was employed by the wealthy businessman John Kehoe. [42]

Fig. 27. *Anthracite coal art created by Kenneth Veden Patience*
(1903-1970)
(photographed by his daughter Katherine Patience Kennedy 2005)

The fourth and sixth sons, Edgar and Harold, remained at 34 Washington Street to follow in their father's footsteps. For over a decade the two brothers would continue using the same business name their father had originated years before. They sold to novelty and wholesale stores, such as Frederick Job's, Cedar Craft Mart, and Helen's Gift Shop in Wilkes-Barre, as well as to others located in Scranton.

Perhaps the brothers would have continued working together for a lifetime had fate not intervened. Harold was drafted into the United States Army during World War II.

***Fig. 28.** Sgt. Harold Lee Patience, Sr. during World War II (1943)*

After being wounded at Anzio Beachhead, Italy, Harold returned to the coal carving business his father had established. Kenneth then relinquished all of his coal carving business contacts to help his youngest brother become reestablished. [43]

COAL ART

HARRY B. PATIENCE'S SONS

PHONE 1425

34 WASHINGTON STREET

WEST PITTSTON, PA.

Fig. 29. Letterhead of the 34 Washington Street Coal Carving Business

Fig. 30. Harold and Edgar Patience working together in "The Shop" circa 1945 (courtesy of Nancy Judge Ardoline)

While Harold was away at war, Edgar had carried on their father's business. However, he had become dissatisfied with simply making coal souvenirs in assembly-line fashion. One reason was because other carvers in the area were stiff competitors for the market and the business of Harry B. Patience's Sons did not have the necessary equipment for mass production.

Fig. 31. *Actual size anthracite charms manufactured by C. Edgar Patience circa 1943*

What Edgar really aspired to do was to sculpt custom-made pieces of art. That was his dream.

A local reporter sometime in the future would write concerning my father's aspirations: *"Patience's work bridges the gap from craftsman to artist. As we contemplate a completed work of art, we may forget that an artist must first be a skilled craftsperson, deeply familiar with the materials and the means of modifying them, in order to make possible the creation of art—the unique expression of the ideas of the artist in such a way as to capture the imagination and emotions of the viewer."* [44]

Fig. 32. *"George Washington," first sculpture circa 1942*
22 ½"" high x 16 wide" x 11 ½"depth

Not until his marriage in 1948 to former World War II WAC Alice Marie Patterson, and after moving his business to Wilkes-Barre, would Edgar be able to fulfill his dream of becoming a sculptor. A Bennett College, Greensboro, N.C., and a Scranton University graduate, Alice was employed as the first African American manager of the Customer Infor-Center of Blue Cross of Northeastern Pennsylvania. [45] Since she was able to provide much of the family income, Edgar then could devote long hours to his art.

Fig. 33. Alice Marie Patterson at age 82, after becoming blind
(1916-2001)
(photo by Mark Danko 1998)

C. Edgar Patience built a small shop at 82 Loomis Street, his wife's family home in Wilkes-Barre. It was just large enough to accommodate the necessary drills, wheels, lathes, saws, and other machinery required for fulfilling his dream. A well-lit display room also was added for persons wishing to purchase unique pieces of art from the anthracite coal region of Pennsylvania.

A self-taught artist, my father studied the works of various sculptors by pouring through books of art and also by visiting museums. One artist he especially admired was Henry Moore whose works he studied at the Museum of Modern Art in New York City. [46] However, nearly ten years were to pass before sculpting would become lucrative; for not until the late 1950s would the work of Charles Edgar Patience become critically acclaimed.

Fig. 34. 82 Loomis Street, Wilkes-Barre, Pa.
(Photo by Mark Danko 1998)

CHAPTER 5
Highest Quality Anthracite

My father was well aware that the anthracite coal from local horizontal veins of the Northern Coal Field of Pennsylvania [47] did not have the right density for sculpting. By many trials and errors he had reached the conclusion that the best coal for his art was located south of Wilkes-Barre in the lower anthracite regions of Schuylkill County where the coal lay in vertical rather than horizontal veins.

"Lower area coal is more compacted by its perpendicular position," he explained. *"It's millions of years in the making."* [48]

So several times a month he would go foraging for the highest quality "black diamonds" he might find at the Mammoth Vein near Hazelton. A meticulous artist, C. Edgar Patience insisted on carving only superior anthracite to attain the best shine when polished with jewelers' rouge and then buffed. He was aware that he might find only one suitable lump out of the thousands he would examine because coal develops flaws as materials leech out of it. Therefore, he had to discover any such flaws first and then try to work around them. [49]

As my father explained his *modus operandus*:

"The primary step is procurement of material. In these preliminary observations concerning the history of anthracite coal, its varying qualities, and natures, the problems in the commercial mining of the product, the marketing, etc. are the total pictures of our local industry.

The material we require for our best work is the rarest of all forms of coal and quite a phenomenon as nature's materials go. Familiar to a few sectors of the anthracite region, there seemed to have occurred deposits of the materials spread over vast areas by the glaciers. Valleys, knolls, hills, and mountains could not resist for long the glaciers' onslaught. Huge basins of craters, once deep swamp recesses, were covered in rare instances with what may have been molten forms of vegetation, rock, etc. until the density of such fill and its subsequent transformation became virtual cores of almost pure anthracite. It is estimated that the final coal formation is about one twentieth of the material originally accumulated.

In the normal process of mining, pockets of this rare material are encountered in specific areas with rare frequency. Because of its rigid and tough nature, this coal is not as responsive to blasting as many other types encountered most frequently. Extra charges of powder are required to dislodge coal in these areas and as a result much splintering and crushing occurs, rendering a very limited amount usable when it is finally made available.

Because of the commercial nature of the mines and breakers, limited time can profitably be devoted to selecting the desired material for ornaments. All mine officials have cooperated in making it possible to select from loaded cars or stock piles of mined coal, but it has been an impractical situation to go into the mine chambers themselves to select and procure from these rare gems of deposits.

As a result, procurement remains the #1 problem. Once material is procured... divesting blocks of coal of the impurities which will adversely affect the final finished appearance is the first step. From what remains after this purging process: hacking, chiseling, any feasible manner, determines size and shape of the article to be finished.

Examining the cleaved chips or the grain structure of blocks determine procedures:

Chips are cut on abrasive wheels to shape and ultimately polish by buffing. Groups of formal shapes are made by slicing blocks of pure unmarked coal and shaping by abrasive cutters... drilling, grooving, fluting, notching. Coal responds as most other materials. The preparation of finish or final buffing is the success or failure of the product.

Lathes, drill presses, grinders, saws, all the tools of the machine shop are used in some instances to facilitate the work. However, the most acclaimed work of all has had a modicum of machine process work and the greatest expression of individual talent.

Our present free forms are a way of returning to the heart of Anthracite with a simple rich style giving utility and versatility to the product." [50]

He explained that compared with some softer stones used for sculpting, coal is able to last as long as pottery and not deteriorate because of atmospheric conditions.

"I still have some pieces that my father carved 50 or 60 years ago." Edgar had said. *"They're still in good condition."* [51]

Fig. 35. Shaving mug carved by Harry B. Patience prior to 1926
Fig. 36. Toothpick holder carved by Harry B. Patience prior to 1926
(both property of author)

Fig. 37. A desk set carved by Harry B. Patience
Fig. 38. "Pansies" 3½" x 2 ½" etched by Harry B. Patience
(both property of author)

Chapter 6

1930s

C. Edgar Patience was commissioned in 1934 to create a coal reproduction of the Model 800 Hoover vacuum cleaner. The forty-one and one half pound replica was presented to the Hoover Company in association with Wilkes-Barre's District 326 "coal-crackers." [52] In the *Ibasaic* newsletter, [53] the name of the sculptor was not mentioned, although it stated that he had worked on it for three weeks from ten to twelve hours per day. [54] The anthracite vacuum was housed at the Hoover Company Archives in Canton, Ohio. [55]

***Fig. 39.** Photograph of "Hoover Vacuum Cleaner"*
(courtesy of the Anthracite Heritage Museum)

The prolific work of the Patience coal carvers has been documented throughout the years in numerous newspaper and magazine articles. One of the earliest appeared in 1938 concerning an exhibit at the Osterhout Public Library on North Franklin Street in Wilkes-Barre, Pennsylvania.

"The objects carved from coal are as slick and shiny as patent leather and include a clock, a pair of black diamond earrings inset with white diamonds, a powder box, crosses, plaques marked with 'Wilkes-Barre' and 'Scranton' and bearing typical coal community scenes, and a miniature mine mule. One of the patient craftsmen has been working on the latter object for five months. It is still dull and scratchy of surface, but will be smooth as satin when finished." [56]

***Fig. 40.** Patent leather slick shiny anthracite art by Harry B. Patience's Sons*

Describing one of the earliest Patience sculptures, a 1939 newspaper article was titled, "There's Some Anthracite to See At The World's Fair."

"For sheer beauty and artistry, it is unlikely that an exhibit in the section of the World's Fair devoted to the hard coal industry will match the handiwork of two West Pittston young men who have just completed a scale model in anthracite of the internationally known Trylon and Perisphere." [57]

My father and his youngest brother Harold had spent a month constructing the model of the 1939 World's Fair theme, Trylon and Perisphere. The newspaper reporter suggested that the surname "Patience" embodied the virtue required for the completion of such a daunting feat.

Created exactly to scale, the model measured almost two feet from the base to the top of the Trylon, an obelisk carved from a single piece of anthracite. From another piece weighing 60 pounds, the polished circular base was cut and shaped to twenty inches in diameter and three inches in depth.

Six inches in diameter, the round Perisphere held the anti-cline (circular ramp) that extended thirty-one inches. The two brothers explained that the most difficult task was fashioning the circular anti-cline from a single piece of coal. Finished in a brighter hue than ebony, the anthracite replica of the Trylon and Perisphere was one of the main items of interest in the anthracite exhibit.

Following the close of the World's Fair, the sculpture sat in my father's office for a number of years where as a child I remember seeing it on his desk. Somehow it was broken, but how, I have no idea. Fortunately, I found a dated photograph of the anthracite Trylon and Perisphere with details about the work of the two Patience carvers. [58]

Fig. 41. C. Edgar Patience at age 33

**Fig. 42.** *"Trylon and Perisphere" exhibited at the 1939 World's Fair (joint project of brothers Edgar and Harold Patience)*

CHAPTER 7
1950s

THE ALTAR IN THE KING'S COLLEGE CHAPEL

The anthracite altar in a small meditation chapel located at the back of the Chapel of Christ the King, King's College, Wilkes-Barre, Pennsylvania, was a 1956 gift from the six sons and three daughters of the Corgan family in memory of their parents, Mr. and Mrs. John B. Corgan, Sr. The 4200-pound piece of anthracite serves as a memorial to the generation that worked in the coal mines in order to provide an education for their children. A request for such a memorial had been made in 1953 by the president of the college, Rev. Leo F. Flood, C.S.C., [59] since King's College had purchased its main building from the Lehigh Valley Coal Company. [60]

Two years were to pass during which three gigantic pieces of anthracite were examined for the ambitious project. However, the first two proved unsatisfactory, but finally an ideal one was excavated from the Wanamie Colliery on the property of the Glen Alden Coal Company in Newport Township. The piece was sent first to the French Creek Granite Company at St. Peters, Pennsylvania, in Chester County. There the top and bottom were cut flat and parallel. [61]

After being commissioned to create the altar, my father would spend a year in designing and executing the project at the Wanamie strippings of the Glen Alden Coal Company. [62] When completed, a beautiful altar measuring 74" x 26" x 37" [63] had been created from the large piece of anthracite. The front and side surfaces of the unique altar dedicated on 21 October 1956 were composed of jewel-like jutting mounds.

On the highly polished centerpiece, my father first with a pencil outlined what he was going to place there. Then with his penknife he meticulously and reverently carved a cross, two anchors, and two Latin inscriptions: *CONGREGATIO A SANCTA CRUCE* and *SPES UNICA*. The first inscription presents the Latin title of the Congregation of Holy Cross, the religions congregation that founded King's College. The cross surmounted at its base by two anchors is their seal and the second inscription their motto, reflecting their conviction that the cross is our "only hope." [64]

Fig. 43: Alice Patience standing in front of the anthracite altar
King's College 1975
Fig. 44: Latin inscription carved on the front of the altar

CHAPTER 8
1960s

STRIKING CHANCEL AREA OF NEW LUTHERAN CHURCH [65]

Newspaper article and photograph:

28 May 1961

"*St. Peter's Lutheran Church, 1000 South Main St., Hanover Township, will be dedicated this morning at 10. Shown is the chancel section of the new church, including a 14-foot carving of "Christ in Blessing" weighing 600 pounds.*

Of striking contemporary design, the church is one of the first in the area featuring a chancel wall constructed almost entirely of mouth blown antique glass of a variety of colors.

The sculpture of Christ, which is suspended in mid-air above the altar, was designed and created especially for the new church in Wisconsin. It arrived on Friday in time for today's dedication.

Another unusual feature of the chancel is the silvered-oak altar which has a facing of 24 blocks of anthracite coal. Fashioned by artist Edgar Patience of Wilkes-Barre, the anthracite pieces represent the altars of stone built by God's people in Old Testament times. Original stock of coal from which the finished blocks were made weighed over five tons. The 24 blocks weigh slightly less than two tons."

Fig. 45*. Twenty-four anthracite bricks compose the altar at St. Peter's Lutheran Church, Hanover, Pa. (photo by LeRoy Patience 2004)*

Fig. 46. "Christ in Blessing" Altar in Chancel of St. Peter's Lutheran
Church, Hanover Township, Pa. (photo by LeRoy Patience 2004)

HALL OF COAL PLANNED [66]

Thursday, 15 December 1960

"HALL OF COAL WILL BE OPENED IN WASHINGTON
Residents of coal mining areas particularly are asked to cooperate in the program to obtain old tools and equipment, mine and machinery catalogues, photographs, engineering drawings, pamphlets, books, magazines, and newspaper articles concerned with coal mining in all of its phases...."

The caption under the accompanying photo reads:
"Searching for memorabilia to be exhibited in the Hall of Coal at the Museum of History and Technology now under construction, officials of the Smithsonian Institution visit the new Coal Building in Washington, D.C. Dr. P.W. Bishop, head curator of the Department of Arts and Manufacturers, and his assistant, Dr. Charles O. Houston, Jr., discuss the coal industry's participation in the project with Stephen F. Dunn, president of the National Coal Association."

◆◆◆

A three-and-one-half ton piece of anthracite, one of the largest ever removed from any mine or stripping operation, was shipped from Wyoming Valley to Washington, D.C., in 1961 for display in a new Arts and Manufacturers Building. Originally weighing four and one-half tons, the mammoth lump of coal was removed from the Baltimore Vein of Franklin Colliery by No. 1 Contracting Company. Due to its huge size, the rare "black diamond" had to be jockeyed out of the face of the mine stripping with the use of an enormous dragline.

Several months prior, coalmine owner Louis Pagnotti had received a letter from Dr. Carl Houston, Jr. of the Department of Arts and Manufacturers. The letter explained that he was seeking an unusual type of exhibition for the new Arts and Manufacturers Building in Washington, D.C., soon to be opened by the Smithsonian Institution.

Inspired, Louis Pagnotti began to search for a rare anthracite specimen suitable for display in the Capitol. Such a piece eventually was discovered hundreds of feet below the surface in the stripping operation along the Ashley Bypass. After Louis Pagnotti had the block removed, it was transported to his Sullivan Trail Shops on Exeter

Avenue in West Pittston where the necessary hydraulic and pneumatic equipment was located for "dressing" the specimen. Because he was aware of C. Edgar Patience's King's College Chapel altar, Louis Pagnotti telephoned the sculptor to ask if he would be interested in preparing a mammoth piece of anthracite for the Smithsonian Institution in Washington, D.C. Of course, my father was interested.

During three weeks of steady labor, he prepared the enormous piece for shipment to the nation's capitol. His first step was to sand and buff it, leaving the sides in a natural stippled state for revealing how anthracite looks when first blasted from veins in the mines. The reflective top surface was to have a mirror-like finish and since anthracite is so easily fractured, my father had to polish it by hand.

After being rolled out of the West Pittston Shops on a specially laid track, the anthracite was hoisted by crane to a flatbed truck whose destination was Washington, D.C. [67] Charles Edgar Patience and his admirers were delighted at the prospect of his work sitting just inside the door of the new Mining and Minerals Industries Hall of Coal at the Smithsonian Institution in the nation's capitol.

Fig.47. *C. Edgar Patience polishing the surface of the monolith planned for the Smithsonian Institution in Washington, D.C. (photo by Lukasik 1961)*

Throughout the years, members of the Patience family, as well as interested others, have been pondering the whereabouts of the gigantic piece of coal. So after moving to the Washington, D.C. area in 1992, I seriously began trying to find out what had happened to the monolith after it reached the Capitol in 1961. Finally, in 2004, someone at the Smithsonian Institution tracked it down for me.

What has come to light is that instead of its being on public display as planned, it never was viewed at all because plans for the new building never reached fruition. Instead, the gigantic piece has been sitting in a Smithsonian storage facility for these many years. [68]

Eventually, I was able make an appointment to see for myself the anthracite piece about which I had heard, read, and seen in photographs, but never had actually observed. Noting that it is covered with a veritable mantle of dust, I perceive that all the "Pennsylvania black diamond" needs is a good shower to be restored to its original gleaming beauty.

Newspaper articles still include the fact that the anthracite monolith is at the Smithsonian Institution. That much is true. However, what has not been included, of course, is the newly discovered fact that it reposes not in the Smithsonian Institution in Washington, but in Maryland where no one can view it without special permission.

Fig. 48. Juanita Patience Moss standing behind the monolith at the Suitland, Md., Storage Facility (photo by Reba Burruss-Barnes 2005)

During this decade of the 60s, interested buyers began collecting the work of C. Edgar Patience for displaying in their businesses and private residences.

Fig. 49. (unnamed) Property of Sondra Meyers, Scranton, Pa.
(photo by Warren Rowe 2005)

When commissioned to carve the bulldog mascot for the Mack Truck Company, C. Edgar Patience was up for the challenge. For many years his gleaming finished product sat among other bulldogs in a collection displayed at the Allentown, Pennsylvania, offices. [69]

Fig. 50. Anthracite mascot at the Mack Truck Company offices (photo courtesy of Mack Trucks)

Many times when dignitaries visited Wyoming Valley, C. Edgar Patience would be called upon to create a special one-of-a-kind piece of his anthracite art. He never duplicated his work.

Fig. 51. *Livingston Clewell, Captain Rose, C. Edgar Patience with a paperweight for Northeastern Pennsylvania Anthracite Marines*

Every piece of art my father created in some way would be unique, even nameplates such as those presented to toastmaster John Addy of New York City and Jack Kelly, Jr. of Philadelphia, principal speaker at the second annual sports banquet sponsored by the Wilkes-Barre Chapter of the King's College Alumni. [70] Even Wendell Wilkie who ran against President Franklin Delano Roosevelt in 1940 received a piece of anthracite art created by C. Edgar Patience. [71] Another went to Ted Mack of the "Original Amateur Hour." He was given a lettered plaque when he visited Wilkes-Barre on 12 January 1950.

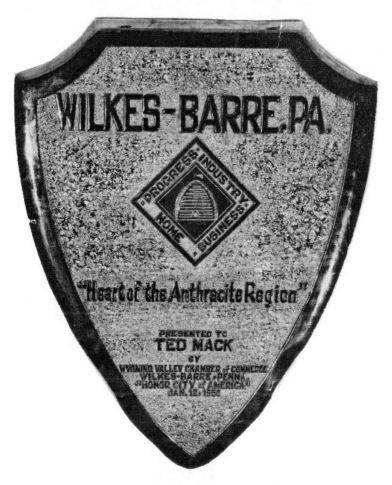

Fig. 52. "Ted Mack" plaque

As a guest of Dr. and Mrs. Eugene Farley, [72] Mrs. Lyndon B. Johnson visited Wilkes-Barre in 1964 for the dedication of a new science building at Wilkes College (now University). A local group presented her with two works of C. Edgar Patience. [73] Several days later he was delighted to receive her letter of thanks.

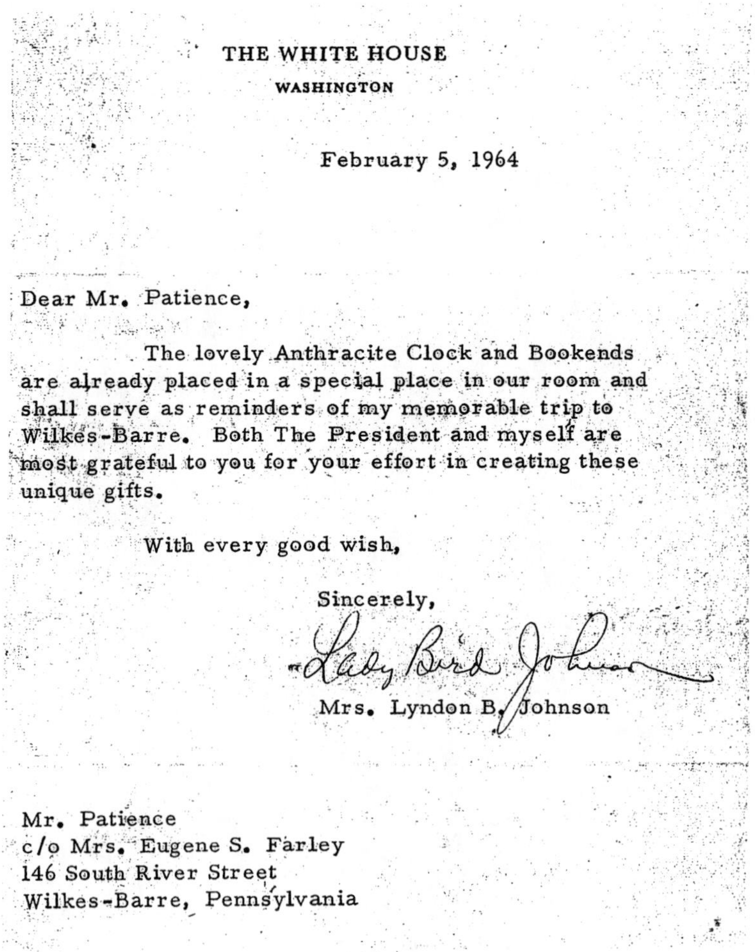

THE WHITE HOUSE
WASHINGTON

February 5, 1964

Dear Mr. Patience,

        The lovely Anthracite Clock and Bookends are already placed in a special place in our room and shall serve as reminders of my memorable trip to Wilkes-Barre. Both The President and myself are most grateful to you for your effort in creating these unique gifts.

        With every good wish,

                Sincerely,

                Lady Bird Johnson

                Mrs. Lyndon B. Johnson

Mr. Patience
c/o Mrs. Eugene S. Farley
146 South River Street
Wilkes-Barre, Pennsylvania

Fig. 53. *"Thank you" letter from Lady Bird Johnson*
(Mrs. Lyndon B. Johnson)

A Wyoming Valley admirer of my father's art was Congressman Daniel Flood (D) who, after having been elected in 1944, continued to represent the 11th Congressional District for thirty-six years. [74] During that period he would present a piece of Patience anthracite art to United States Presidents from Franklin Delano Roosevelt to Richard Nixon. [75] Assistant District Attorney Ernest Preate, Jr. continued the tradition by presenting the sculpture "Anthracite" to President Jimmy Carter in 1977. [76]

To commemorate Congressman Daniel Flood's twentieth year of service, the Belmont Club of Wilkes-Barre presented him with a gift created by C. Edgar Patience. According to a newspaper article, the anthracite desk set occupied a prominent place in the Washington office of the congressman. [77]

DANIEL J. FLOOD
11TH DIST., PENNSYLVANIA

COMMITTEE:
APPROPRIATIONS

Congress of the United States
House of Representatives
Washington, D. C.

WASHINGTON OFFICE:
331 OLD HOUSE OFFICE BLDG.

HOME OFFICE:
1015 MINERS NATIONAL BANK
WILKES-BARRE, PENNSYLVANIA

October 30, 1957

Mr. Harry B. Patience
82 Loomis Street
Wilkes-Barre, Pennsylvania

Dear Mr. Patience:

    I have just returned from a two months' tour of Europe on official business, and while there had a very interesting talk with George Marvin Pollard, Esq., Consul of the United States of America, in Munich, Germany.

    During our conversation he expressed interest in Anthracite souvenirs etc., and I would like to suggest to you to send him your catalogue and information, as he is desirous of obtaining some of these as presents to the Germans.

    Please let me know if and when you have done this.

Sincerely yours,

DANIEL J. FLOOD, M.C.

DJF/hmt

__Fig. 54. A Letter from Congressman Daniel Flood__

The unique art of C. Edgar Patience has been displayed at various locations outside of the Wyoming Valley and even outside of the United States. My stepmother, Alice Patterson Patience, wrote in her memoirs about one place in particular.

"When Barbados received independence from England in 1966, Edgar was commissioned to make the seal of the new Barbados. He created it in coal and it was very beautiful.

On one of our trips to Barbados he was acknowledged as the person who made the seal and he was honored. The newspapers played up his visit." [78]

Fig. 55. *Anthracite clock presented to Hon. Errol Walton Barrow, the first Prime Minister after Barbados independence in 1966*

◆◆◆

Among the number of craftsmen chosen in 1967 from thirty states to help stimulate travel to Canada, C. Edgar Patience was one of the five Pennsylvanians who were part of the United States display on American folk heritage at the Canada Expo in Montreal. His anthracite art was viewed at the Cooperative Crafts Exhibit sponsored by the U.S. Department of Agriculture.

One evening he was both surprised and pleased when Prime Minister Lester B. Pearson of Canada, along with the press, paid a visit to the booth of C. Edgar Patience where an anthracite bust of President John F. Kennedy was on display. [79] My father had worked on the piece for nine months.

The remarkable likeness, a masterpiece of contrasts from stippled to polished, was being introduced to the public for the first time at the U.S. Travel Service Exhibit at Montreal's continuing Exposition, "Man and His World." Several of my father's abstract pieces shown for the first time at the Expo led to a later display in 1968 at the Joseph Grippi Gallery in New York City. [80]

Fig. 56. Anthracite Bust of President John F. Kennedy

◆◆◆

First Lady Mrs. Richard M. Nixon was photographed in 1969 as she admired a piece of my father's anthracite coal art at the opening program of the Department of Agriculture's Third Annual Cooperative Crafts Exhibit in Washington, D.C. It was an October Co-op Month event being held that year at the U.S. Department of Agriculture.

Following the formal program, Secretary of Agriculture Clifford M. Hardin and Mrs. Hardin accompanied Mrs. Nixon on a tour of the crafts displayed by the cooperatives and guilds of thirty-two states. The photographs including C. Edgar Patience's niece, Betty Patience Claiborne, who also was his frequent assistant, were published in both the *EBONY* and *JET* magazines. [81]

Fig. 57. *Pat Nixon (Mrs. Richard Nixon), C. Hardin, C. Edgar Patience and his niece Betty Patience Claiborne in 1969 (courtesy of EBONY 2006)*

CHAPTER 9

1970s

A four-page March 1970 *EBONY* spread featuring C. Edgar Patience reads: *"He has made a name for himself as one of this nation's most unusual sculptor—creating masterpieces of art from chunks of penny-a pound hard coal."* [82]

Included also in the article was information about the veterans of the 101st Airborne Division returning to Europe to take part in the 25th anniversary celebration of the liberation of Holland from Germany. At that time they presented Queen Juliana of the Netherlands with two of C. Edgar Patience's works: a jeweled clock and an eighteen-inch, 8mm anthracite "pearl" necklace that took forty painstaking hours to create. [83]

Fig. 58. *C. Edgar Patience carving the Latin inscription on the altar in the King's College Chapel, Wilkes-Barre, Pa. (courtesy of EBONY magazine 2006)*

58

The *Lapidary Journal* in the April 1970 issue stated that *"patience is a virtue"* and that *"it is eminently fitting that a man of the black race with the name of Patience should call on his artistic skills to produce beautiful black magic from this thing called coal."* [84] Also a publication for fifth graders, "My Weekly Reader," reported in October of the same year, *"A white haired old man climbs a steep coal hill near Wilkes-Barre, Pennsylvania. He is bent over looking for 'black gems.' He picks up various pieces of anthracite coal. Why? Because he is an artist at work! C. Edgar Patience is a coal sculptor."* [85]

People who were acquainted with my father certainly know that he never thought of himself as being "old." After all, he was only sixty-four years old when the article was published, but to the fifth graders, indeed he was very old, especially with his white hair.

Fig. 59. Charles Edgar Patience at age 60

One of the greatest challenges of my father's career would face him in the fall of 1970 when he agreed to sculpt a likeness of Dr. H. Beecher Charmbury, Pennsylvania Secretary of Mines and Minerals Industries. Colleagues of the veteran state official wanted to surprise him at a testimonial dinner to be held in Scranton. One member of the planning committee suggested that there could be no finer keepsake for Dr. Charmbury than an anthracite likeness of himself.

When first offered the commission, Edgar had been reluctant. Afterwards he admitted, *"I thought it was beyond me. But I was delighted with how it turned out."* [86]

The first challenge, of course, was to find the finest quality anthracite for the project. After searching for several months, a suitable piece finally was located in Schuylkill County at the world's deepest strip mine. [87]

The second challenge was for Dr. Charmbury to be sketched without being discovered, since the gift was to be a surprise. By studying photographs provided by Mrs. Charmbury and by surreptitiously observing his subject at various settings, my father prepared sketches for the bust he was able to complete in two months.

"Although," he said, *"it usually takes me six months to do something like that."* [88]

Dr. Charmbury was delighted to receive his surprise on 9 October 1970 at the Jermyn Inn in Scranton, Pennsylvania. [89] C. Edgar Patience was delighted that he had met the challenge.

Fig. 60. Bust of Dr. H. Beecher Charmbury 1970

During his latter years, C. Edgar Patience was asked to display his work at various venues, including the Dallas Rotary Club's Fall Fair and Lit Brothers exhibit in Philadelphia, both in 1968, and an exhibit during "Festival III" at the Courthouse Square in Scranton in 1970. [90]

Some other exhibits were the "Travel Pennsylvania Show" held at Gimbel's in Philadelphia in 1971, [91] the Palmerton Hospital Festival, and for five consecutive years, the annual Fine Arts Fiesta on the Public Square in Wilkes-Barre.

Fig. 61. Lit Brothers in Philadelphia 1968 (photo by Freedman)

Fig. 62. *Fine Arts Fiesta on Public Square, Wilkes-Barre, Pa. 1970*
(photo by Ace Holman)

"Pennsylvania Excitement" at Gimbel's in 1972 was a panorama of the people, places, and things making the Keystone State a Mecca for vacationers and tourists. The exhibition had returned to the Center City store in Philadelphia for the fourth consecutive year. [92]

The store had staged colorful exhibits on both the first and fifth floors for the dozens of participants who traveled from all regions of Pennsylvania. C. Edgar Patience was among the talented craftsmen and artisans invited from 22-27 May 1972 to display their work.

Fig. 63. Gimbel's in Philadelphia, Pa. 1972

Considerable interest was generated on the fifth floor where C. Edgar Patience's gleaming anthracite coal art was being displayed. *"Is that really coal? Why, it looks just like onyx!"* Those are the first words the artist most often heard when people would lay their astounded eyes on his beautiful art.

Always willing to explain his work, he would point out that coal is a deeper, softer black than onyx while adding, *"You can't take any old lump of furnace coal and turn it into a handsome key chain decoration."* [93]

"Isn't it dirty?" was the other question most frequently asked.

"Well, why don't you rub your hand over a piece and see?" would be the artist's response in anticipation of the surprised look he knew would soon appear.

Even though thought of as just a dirty fuel by many, anthracite coal to my father was a medium for the expression of the unusual and the beautiful. Every item he fashioned, from small sculptures like "Cleopatra" to the 4200-pound coal altar in the chapel at King's College, was hand carved with no two pieces ever being identical. [94]

Fig. 64. *"Cleopatra Gazes at the Pyramids" (property of the author)*

WILKES BARRE SCULPTOR LURES VISITORS [95]

"Recently Tom Alliton called your scribe from New Kensington calling attention to the above headline in the Pittsburgh Press. C. Edgar Patience, the world's foremost sculptor of coal was to exhibit his work at Joseph Horne Department Store for a three-week period starting May 18, 1972. We immediately dashed off an invitation to him to attend our meeting on the 19th. On May 2nd the following reply was received:

Dear Mr. Remele,

Thank you for your kind invitation to be present at your meeting on May 19, 1972. I am extremely sorry that it is not possible for me to attend.

Although the Joseph Horne Company will begin featuring artists and craftsmen early in May, I am not scheduled to be in Pittsburgh until May 30th. My exhibit will continue through June 3. Previous commitments for other shows in our state prevented me from accepting the earlier date.

It is gratifying to know that you are interested in coal sculpture. The articles in the Lapidary Journal describing my work were quite a tribute and I would have enjoyed meeting all of you. Perhaps, something can be arranged at a later date.

Sincerely yours,

C. Edgar Patience

Unknowingly, my father's final exhibit would be the one held at Joseph Horne Company in Pittsburgh. Having arrived there on 29 May 1972, he was very excited because he was going to be interviewed on television for the first time in his career.

Two weeks prior at Gimbel's in Philadelphia, he had been very successful in selling more items than he had anticipated. Therefore, before driving to Pittsburgh, he had to spend long hours in his shop to replace his inventory. Unfortunately, he caught a cold. Five years before when he had a bout with pneumonia, his physician had warned that due to the damage his lungs had incurred through his lifetime of inhaling coal dust, even a mere cold was dangerous for him.

Since his wife had not been able to leave her job again so soon after assisting him at the Philadelphia show, my father took a friend along to help with the drive over the steep mountains. The Pittsburgh exhibit was successful, too, but my father's cold had worsened and so, by the time his television interview was finished, he was quite ill.

Refusing to be hospitalized in Pittsburgh and insisting that his friend drive him home to Wilkes-Barre, he had developed pneumonia again by the time he reached 82 Loomis Street. Just three days after being admitted to the General Hospital, Charles Edgar Patience died on 7 June 1972 at the age of sixty-five years and ten months.

A local newspaper article read: *"That his work brought him honor is attested in the various tributes. He was named to 'Who's Who In the East,' 'Who's Who in America,'(1972) 'Who's Who in the World.' After his death, Mrs. Patience received word that he had been proposed for inclusion in the next edition of the National Social Directory and the National Register of Prominent Americans and International Notables (1974-1975). Within the past few months he was also included in the 'Wisdom Hall of Fame,' a distinguished honor roll of eminent Americans."* [96]

In a second article, the same staff writer added, *"His catalogue card number at the Library of Congress is 78-75747."* [97]

◆◆◆

During Hurricane Agnes, the deluge pouring down the Susquehanna River from broken dams in the state of New York overflowed the dikes built to protect the city of Wilkes-Barre from inundation. However, they were not nearly high enough to prevent the banks from overflowing early Friday morning, 23 June 1972. [98]

Consequently, Central-City Wilkes-Barre was covered by water to third stories of residences and businesses that had the misfortune of being near the river. For many blocks east of the riverbank, the rising floodwaters of the Susquehanna severely damaged buildings, including the King's College Chapel situated in the lounge between the Main Building and the Science Wing of the school. Fortunately, the anthracite coal altar was not damaged significantly as compared to the rest of the Chapel, including the furniture. However, even though the water level had risen just to touch the base of the unique altar, damage occurred underneath. In addition, on the left side of the altar several threatening cracks appeared from top to bottom. [99]

The devastating Flood of '72 happened just sixteen days after the death of my father. Certainly, had he still been living he would have been asked to assess and to repair the precious anthracite altar. However, C. Edgar Patience was no longer living, having succumbed on the 7th of June.

Consequently, the young coal carver from Plains, Pennsylvania, Frank Magdalinski, was asked to repair the altar. When I asked him to explain for this book just what he had to do, he told me, *"The first time I restored the altar was after the Agnes Flood in 1972. The altar was falling apart due to the aging of the coal and the temperature changes in the room itself.*

Some of three corners were breaking off and seam cracks were getting real huge. I chipped away at least five to six inches all around the original stone and replaced it with coal that was held together using a mixture of coal dust and resin. It was constructed in a way that made it a permanent fixture. In other words, it couldn't be moved without cutting the floor around it." [100]

The altar was restored satisfactorily, continuing then to be used for worship at the King's College Chapel. Concern for it again, though, will be published in the newspapers in 1983 when Frank Magdalinski comes to its rescue one more time.

CHAPTER 10
Posthumous Recognition

PATIENCE EXHIBIT OPENS AT KING'S [101]

12 March 1973

"The week-long memorial showing of the coal sculptures created by the late C. Edgar Patience opened Sunday at King's College with a brief ceremony lauding the artist.

Patience, a Wilkes-Barre resident, gained national and international fame with his moldings, jewelry, and etchings from the mineral that formed the economy of Wyoming Valley.

Mrs. Patience, noting her husband's love for this area and for his work, unveiled the bust of the late Pres. John F. Kennedy, a remarkable likeness chiseled from coal.

Large pieces of sculpture displayed include busts of President Kennedy and President George Washington; Amalarice, the Meek One; Hair; Portrait of a Man; Serenity; Black Friday; Love; Ezekiel's Wheel; Stone Upon Stone; and Coaltown—USA, the most unusual item in the collection representing a mining town of 25 to 50 years ago."

Fig. 65. *"Stone Upon Stone"*

More than 9,000 persons were reported in attendance at the memorial show held at King's College Library where the art of Charles Edgar Patience was displayed and sold. [102] The desire of his widow was for people and businesses to acquire his work so it will be preserved for the admiration of future generations.

Representative Daniel Flood had planned to open the exhibit, but was detained in Washington, D.C. However, he sent a telegram *"lauding the unique work that ceased with the death of its creator."* [103]

Hosting the program was Rev. Lane Kilburn, C.S.C., the president of King's College. Many dignitaries were in attendance when the bust of President John F. Kennedy was unveiled, later purchased by someone whose name I have not been able to find among my father's records.

◆◆◆

Representative Joseph Semanoff of Leighton, Pennsylvania, was named Honorary Ambassador of Good Will to Holland in 1973. At that time he presented Queen Juliana of the Netherlands with another anthracite sculpture by C. Edgar Patience. [104]

◆◆◆

BUT CALLS IT NOT STRICT ENOUGH [105]

August 1977
"Anthracite," a coal sculpture of stippled coal (the natural state) with the surface smoothed and engraved, was purchased from Edgar's widow and presented to President Jimmy Carter by Assistant District Attorney Ernest D. Preate, Jr. The occasion was the signing one of the nation's first surface mining laws. After seven years of legislative struggles among Congress and battles between the mining industry and environmental interest, the bill was finally signed in a Rose Garden ceremony.

The bill bans ripping through the surface of land that cannot be reclaimed, requires mining companies to restore land that can be reclaimed, and imposes a tax of 35 cents on a ton of strip mined coal and 15 cents on a ton of deep mined coal to pay for the restoration.

However, President Carter said the bill was not strict enough to force coal companies to restore all of the new land they ravage and to pay for repairs for the damage they had done in the past. 'I am concerned with some of the features that had to be watered down to get it passed.'"

LATE EDGAR PATIENCE GAINS SCULPTURE HONOR [106]

....11 November 1978

"Additional honors are being heaped—posthumously—on the late C. Edgar Patience, 82 Loomis Street, Wilkes-Barre, who gained the reputation of being one of the two recognized coal artists in the world.

Tuesday, William J. Wewer, executive director of the Pennsylvania Historical and Museum Commission and William N. Richards, director of the Bureau of Museums for the Commission, visited Patience's widow.

They expressed the intent to acquire 'Coaltown—USA' and the 'Bust of George Washington' for the collections of the commission...."

Fig. 66. *"Coaltown—USA" 9" height x 16 ¼" width x 11" depth at the Anthracite Heritage Museum (photo by Reba Burruss-Barnes 2004)*

When the Afro-American Historical and Cultural Museum in Philadelphia, Pennsylvania, held an exhibit in 1981, the only sculpture displayed was "Amalarice" by C. Edgar Patience. The caption in the exhibit's catalog reads, *"Edgar Patience's anthracite coal sculptures are among the most unusual and moving works of modern art."* [107]

Fig. 67. *"Amalarice" 12 ¾" height x 7 ¾" width x 9" diameter*
at the Anthracite Heritage Museum (photo by Reba Burruss-Barnes 2004)

"KING'S COLLEGE (GENTLY) MOVES COAL ALTAR" [108]

.....*Thursday, 18 August 1983*

<u>Photo caption</u>- "*Workmen Maneuver 4,000-pound altar*"

"*Although coal is selling for approximately $60 a ton these days, there was quite a bit of concern over moving two tons of coal at King's College on Tuesday. The coal in question was the 4000-pound anthracite coal altar which was moved to a temporary home in the Scanlon Physical Education Center until the college's new Chapel of Christ the King and Campus Ministry are completed early next year.*

The altar was the dream of former King's President Rev. Leo Flood, C.S.C. (1950-1955), now residing in St. Petersburg, Florida. The dream became a reality in 1955 when the Glen Alden Coal Company, through the generosity of the Corgan Family of Kingston, presented King's with the 10x4x2 foot altar (correction- 74'' x 26'' x 37 ½'').

.   *The altar (which has an additional 1000 pound marble top) is the largest of his works.*

The altar was moved once before in 1971 to its present site by the Lavette Transport Company (correction- Lavelle's Express). *It's formal dedication at the college was Oct. 21, 1956, and it has been a landmark and topic of conversation to all visitors to the King's campus.*"

◆◆◆

Once again coal carver Frank Magdalinski was called upon to help save the altar. "*When King's College built a new chapel, an attempt to move the coal altar from the main building to the chapel proved to be disastrous. The coal I replaced in 1972 around the original piece that your Dad did, was destroyed.*

Since the altar was going to be placed against a wall, only three sides had to be replaced. This time I used a ¾ inch plywood as a backing to adhere the lumps of coal. After pre-fitting the plywood to the plywood to the altar to make sure that it was a correct fit, I did most of the work at my plant so all I had to do was assemble the three sides on site. Using metal rods sort of like huge toggle bolts, it took two months to do the reconstruction and about two weeks to assemble it at the chapel." [109]

Even after thirty-four years since the death of C. Edgar Patience, Wyoming Valley newspaper articles still are being written about his art. Because he was an African American, interest in him often accelerates during February, designated as Black History Month. During that month, for instance, "For Kids Today," recently printed the following lines:

HARD COAL FUELED HIS DREAMS [110]

"Down, down, down, C. Edgar Patience used to descend into gloomy shafts.

But the Wilkes-Barre man wasn't a miner. He was an artist who collected his raw material—anthracite coal—directly from its source.

Other people might have said coal was just a rock that you could burn in a stove or a furnace, a cheap fuel you could use to bake a pie or heat your home.

But to his artist's eye, Patience saw in coal the potential for something more.

He knew that by carving, chiseling, sanding, and polishing he could sculpt those lumps of carbon into pieces of art that would amaze and dazzle.

Visit the Pennsylvania Anthracite Heritage Museum in Scranton, and you'll see three samples of his work from the 1950's and '60s..."

Commonwealth of Pennsylvania
Pennsylvania Historical and Museum Commission

Anthracite Museum Complex

Pennsylvania Anthracite Heritage Museum
R.D. 1, Bald Mountain Road
Scranton, PA 18504
(570) 963-4804
Fax (570) 963-4194

Epilogue

I cannot close this book without telling you about a recent serendipitous incident concerning my father and his work. It began like this.

After moving to Virginia from New Jersey in 1992, I became a member of a local alumnae chapter of the sorority to which I belong, Delta Sigma Theta, Inc. In 2003 I was asked if I would donate the historical novel I had written, *Created to Be Free*, for a silent auction at a fundraising gala. I was happy to do so; and in order to stimulate interest in the bidding that evening, I stood near my book to explain why I had written it, and, of course, why I thought people should bid on it.

The bidding went very well, beyond the original price of the book. So, being satisfied, I entered the area where the entertainment for the evening was being held.

Upon entering the room, I immediately spied a chapter member whom I had not seen in a number of years. She, too, is an author and at her book signing several years prior, I had told her that I was writing a book about my great grandfather. She told me to be sure to notify her when I had completed it.

After spotting me, she waved me over to her table and then proceeded to apologize for not having purchased my book yet. I responded enthusiastically with, "Well, you certainly are in luck. You have your chance tonight. The book is out in the other room. Come on. You can bid on it."

We then left the room and walked toward the table where *Created to Be Free* was propped up for display. From the distance my friend was peering at the book very intently. Then when we were standing right in front of it, she turned to me and asked, "Is 'Patience' your middle name or your last name?"

"My last name."

In her very soft voice she continued, "Umm. I used to know a man whose last name was Patience." Then she asked, "Where are you from?"

"West Pittston, Pennsylvania."

She thought for a second before replying, "No, that's not it."

"How about Wilkes-Barre, Pennsylvania?"

"Yes, that's it," she affirmed. "He made beautiful things out of coal."

Quite flabbergasted, I inquired of her, "How did you know my father?"

She responded with her sweet smile, "I wrote the *EBONY* article about him."

At that point I let out a loud exclamation. The people all around us must have thought I had lost my mind.

Why had we never made the connection before this time? After all, we had known each other for several years. The reason is quite simple.

Carolyn DuBose's by-line had not been published with the March 1970 *EBONY* feature that is so precious to my family. Besides that, I never had gone by Juanita <u>Patience</u> Moss until I began writing my books. Talk about a small world!

EBONY MAGAZINE
March 1970

COAL-BLACK ART

Sculptor created masterpieces from penny-a-pound anthracite.

"A lone figure bends over a workbench in the shadowy confines of a narrow room filled with dust and grime. Breathing through a surgeon's mask, C. Edgar Patience is oblivious to his surroundings. For here, in this little world of his own in Wilkes-Barre, Pa., he has made a name for himself as one of the nation's most unusual sculptors—creating masterpieces of art from chunks of penny-a-pound hard coal... " [111]

Fig. 68. EBONY *writer Carolyn DuBose at an anthracite colliery while interviewing C. Edgar Patience in 1969 (courtesy of Carolyn DuBose, photo by Sorrell)*

C. EDGAR PATIENCE
Anthracite Coal Carving
82 LOOMIS STREET
WILKES-BARRE, PENNA.

PHONE VA 2-5526

March 17, 1970.

Mrs. Carolyn Du Bose
Ebony
Washington, D.C.

Dear Mrs. Du Bose,

If I were able fully to write the words to express my joy all the way to "Cloud Nine" I just might have your kind of a job! Yes, the suspense was agonizing but when the advance copy came — well, it was worth all. Please accept my gratitude for that beautiful feature story. Wilkes-Barre's supply for the news stands was exausted vertually over night so numbers of people including us resorted to getting copies through New York friends. Letters and phone calls are coming in from many friends and former customers day after day.

Can I buy any of Mr. Sorrell's pictures? Some men are looking for their picture in the story almost as if to find them between the single sheets! (Joke maybe??) Regards to that genius of photography. Regards to your family.

Fondly and respectfully
C. Edgar Patience

Fig. 69. *"Thank you" letter from C. Edgar Patience to Carolyn DuBose*

Appendix I

TABLE No. 5.—List of Non-Fatal accidents that occurred in and about the mines of the Third Anthracite Mine District, for the year ending December 31, 1896.

Date of accident	Number of accident	Name of Person	Occupation	Age	Married	Number of children	Name of Colliery	Location	Nature and Cause of Accident
Jan. 3,	1	Lewis Siashinsky,	Miner,	31	S.		Schooley shaft,	Exeter,	Bruised by fall of rock.
4,	2	John Padinarik,	Miner,	23	S.		East Boston shaft,	Kingston township,	Head cut by fall of rock.
4,	3	Enoch Miller,	Driver,	28	S.	4	Stevens slope,	Exeter,	Both legs broken by hav'ng been caught between car bumpers.
4,	4	John Skonl1,	Miner,	32	S.		Exeter shaft,	Exeter,	Head and face cut; went back to a blast he thought had failed.
7,	5	Lewis V'skcooki,	Laborer,	23	M.		Henry shaft,	Plains township,	These two men were painfully injured by fall of rock while loading a car.
7,	6	Michael Dooly,	Laborer,	40	M.	2	Henry shaft,	Plains township,	
8,	7	Jas Sheratn,	Laborer,	32	M.	2	Babylon shaft,	Duryea,	Foot painfully injured. He drove a pick into it.
10,	8	Edward Naugle,	Gate tender,	17	S.		Butler breaker,	Pittston township,	Hand crushed.
15,	9	Harry Pattenie,	Laborer,	17	S.		Exeter breaker,	Exeter,	Arm painfully squeezed by having been caught in conveyors.
15,	10	Michael Healey,	Miner,	49	M.		Consolidated slope,	Avoca,	Father and son were severely injured by fall of soapstone.
15,	11	Michael Healey,	Laborer,	24	S.		Consolidated slope,	Avoca,	
16,	12	Charles Coupris,	Miner,	55	M.	7	East Boston shaft,	Kingston township,	Head and leg bruised by fall of checker coal.
20,	13	Geo. Carr,	Miner,	42	M.	3	Mill Hollow shaft,	Luzerne,	Painfully bruised by fall of bony coal.
21,	14	James Smith,	Runner,	23	S.		Henry shaft,	Plains township,	Squeezed while coupling cars.
23,	15	Andrew Moscow,	Runner,	30	M.		Phoenix breaker,	Duryea,	Severely squeezed between cars while coupling them.
24,	16	Robt. Deckell,	Miner,	23	M.	3	Babylon shaft,	Duryea,	Side injured by a piece of rock falling on him.
27,	17	Archie Stanton,	Track man,	28	M.	3	Babylon shaft,	Duryea,	Leg broken by a fall of rock.
27,	18	Anthony Broshick,	Laborer,	28	M.		Mill Hollow shaft,	Luzerne,	Severely bruised by coal sliding off the gob on him.
29,	19	Anthony Kane,	Driver boss,	30	S.		Twin shaft,	Pittston,	Slightly burned and bruised by an explosion of gas.
30,	20	Peter Larke,	Driver,	17	S.		Clear Spring shaft,	Pittston,	Leg broken; fell under trip of empty cars.

*Fig. 70. Early work of Harry B. Patience circa 1900
Stick pins in middle, hat pins on right*

Appendix II

What Are Pennsylvania Diamonds.

Scientists Explain

how Iron and Sulphur are dissolved by the water percolating through coal beds and carrying them along a sloping plane of roof or under surfade until a warmer current of air is met with which claims it's share of the water, and there being then more Iron and Sulphur than the remaining water can carry, it deposits the excess upon the roof or under surface of the incline plane and now begins the building up of the little cubes, piled one upon the other, their sizes varying as varies the current of air beneath or the amount of material held in solution, but building, ever building such pretty gems as the hand of man has never been able to produce, and thus we get a glance into nature's workshop, where the cunning artificers are the simple elements toiling in the depth of darkness, into which no ray of sunshine ever penetrates. .   . .   .

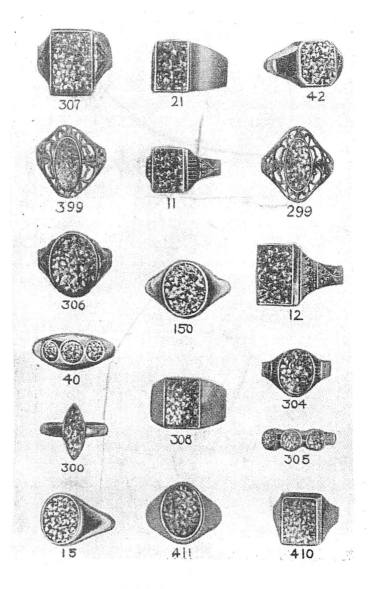

Monel metal [(112)] rings with "Pennsylvania diamond" settings catalog of Frederick Job Manufacturing and Wholesale circa 1920 198 & 200 S. Main St., Wilkes-Barre, Pa.

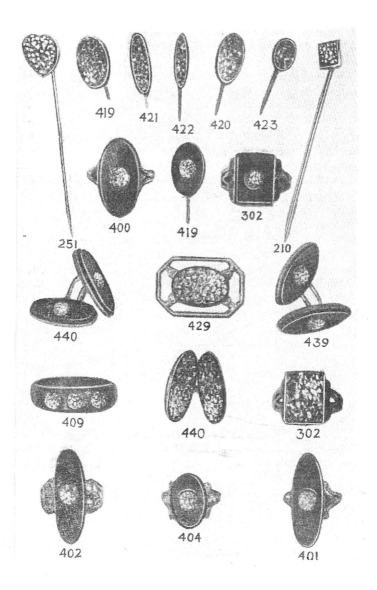

Work of Harry B. Patience's Sons circa 1920
from catalog of Frederick Job Manufacturing and Wholesale

Appendix III

PRICE - LIST.

SULPHUR SETTING

No. of Article		Price
161	Charms round 1 setting	$0.50
162	Charms round 1 setting scalloped edge	"0.75
163	Charms round 7 settings	"1.00
164	Hearts small 1 setting	"0.50
27	Hearts medium 1 setting	"0.75
166	Hearts medium large 6 settings	"1.20
68	Hearts large 10 settings	"2.00
61	Stick pins for men	"0.50
60	Stick pins bangle for ladies	"0.50
3	Beauty pins round	"0.50
64	Breast pins oblong	"1.00
76	Fobs ladies 4 pieces joined together	"2.00
152	Fobs gents 4 pieces joined together	"2.25
72	Bracelets 10 pieces joined	"3.25
71	Necklaces 24 pieces joined	"8.00
59	Cuff links	"1.25
79	Earrings, clamp	"1.25
78	Earrings, screw	"1.25
92	Hat pins, acorn 1 setting	"0.40
9	Hat pins oval 1 setting	"0.50
85	Hat pins, square 1 setting	"0.50
83	Hat pins, oval 5 settings	"1.25
80	Hat pins, square 5 settings	"1.25
81	Hat pins, 1 large setting	"0.75
58	Charm small	"0.50

Price list from catalog of Harry B. Patience's Sons circa 1920

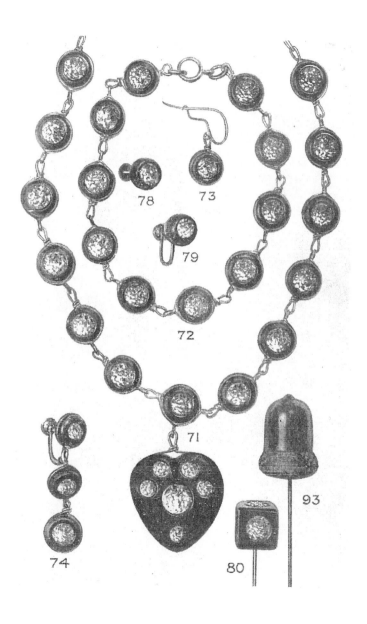

Jewelry from catalog of Harry B. Patience's Sons circa 1920

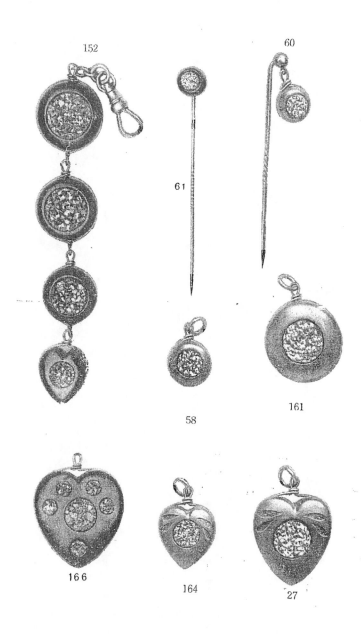

Jewelry from catalog of Harry B. Patience's Sons circa 1920

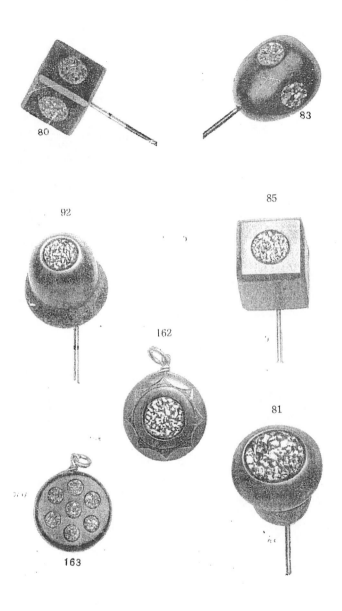

Jewelry from catalog of Harry B. Patience's Sons circa 1920

From catalog of Harry B. Patience's Sons circa 1920

Appendix IV

SOME WORKS OF CHARLES EDGAR PATIENCE

"Abraham Lincoln"
African masks
"Amalarice"
"Ancient Love"
"Anthracite"
Ashtrays
Baseball and Football Trophies
"Bear"
"Black Friday"
"Black Hand"
Bookends
"Boxing Gloves"
"Butterfly"
Candle holders
"Cat"
"Basket"
"Chess Pieces"
"Cleopatra"
Clocks
"Coaltown"
"Coal Shuttle" Trophy
Desk Sets
"Distelfink"
"Dolphin"
"Dr. Charmbury"
"Egg"
"Elephant"
Etchings
"Ezekiel's Wheel"
"Flight"
"Forest Scene"
"Four Seasons"
"George Washington"
"Geos"
"Hair"
"Hoover Vacuum Cleaner"
"In a Grecian Garden"

Jewelry
"Kennedy"
King's College Chapel Altar
"King Tut"
Lamp Bases
Letter Openers
"Love"
Mack Truck "Bulldog"
"Madonna"
"Mama"
"Midsummer's Night Dream"
"Miner"
Monolith at Anthracite Museum
Monolith at Smithsonian
Name Plaques
"Nativity"
"Owl"
"Panther"
Paper Weights
Pincushion Holders
"Piper"
"Portrait of a Man"
"Sea Shell"
"September Morn"
"Serendipity"
"Serenity"
"Shall We Dance?"
Shaving Mugs
"SHE"
"Slave Girl"
St. Peter's Lutheran Church Altar
Statues
"Stone on Stone"
Toothpick holders
"Trylon and Perisphere"
"Upward"
Vases
"Warrior Prince"

Fig. 71. A collage of anthracite art by C. Edgar Patience

Fig. 72. A gleaming ashtray (property of author)
__Fig. 73__. Anthracite candleholder (Betty Patience Claiborne Collection)
Anthracite Heritage Museum, Scranton, Pa.

Fig. 74. C. Edgar Patience carving "Coaltown—USA" circa 1971, an unfinished work

Appendix V

Who's Who In America 1972

"Patience, Charles Edgar

Sculptor, b. W. Pittston, Pa., Aug. 27, 1906, s. Harry and Elsie (Miller) P., grad. high sch; mar. Alice Marie Patterson, Sept. 16, 1948; children- Juanita B. (Mrs. Edward I. Moss), Etta P. (Mrs. Arthur Brown), Harry B.

Exhibitions, Anthracite coal sculptures include Joseph Grippi Gallery, N.Y.C., 1968, Gimbel's, Phila. 1969-70, Lit Bros., Phila., 1969, Dept. Agr. Coop. Exhibit, Washington, D.C. 1969, Fine Arts Fiesta, Wilkes-Barre, PA, 1965-70, also schools, churches, YW-YMCAs.

Prime works include altar at King's College, monolith at William Penn Museum, Harrisburg, sculptured display lamp at Smithsonian Ins. Past Pres. Showcase Theater. Bd. Directors, Art Council, Masons, Club 402 (bd. of govs.), Wilkes-Barre Luzerne-Lackawanna Boosters (past pres.).

(Wilkes-Barre Scranton address. 82 Loomis St. Wilkes-Barre, PA 18702)" [113]

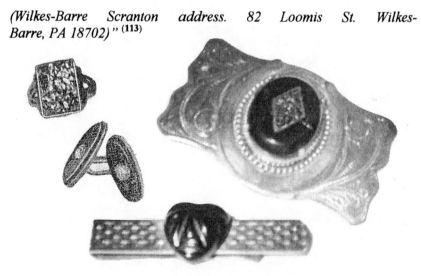

Fig. 75. Men's jewelry

**Fig. 76**. C. Edgar Patience sculpting in his Wilkes-Barre shop circa 1970

Appendix VI

In Memorium

ANTHRACITE VALLEY NEWS

by Rena Baldrica

"A few words to honor the memory of a wonderful man. The late Charles Edgar Patience was an exceptional, talented artist. His hands molded unusual articles from anthracite coal what God gifted him to see with his mind's eye. He nurtured and cultivated his ideas and achieved the success his dreams permitted.

When he talked to you about his work with a rugged piece of black coal, the light in his eyes brought out what was in his heart.

His love for and pride in his work can be seen at the King's College Chapel—the altar he sculptured from anthracite weighing 4,000 pounds. The other local work of art is the Emblem Plaque, molded from coal and put in the Musto clinic at Wilkes-Barre General Hospital. I remember that he remarked how pleased he was to mold this piece of coal, because the late Rep. James Musto fought and gave his life for the miner who worked with coal.

Pennsylvania has lost a unique artist. I in turn pay my personal tribute to a man I admired—Mr. Charles Edgar Patience. May he be with God." [(114)]

Fig. 77. *"Keystone State," the Commonwealth of Pennsylvania*

EULOGY [(115)]

10 June 1972

Charles Edgar Patience, one of six sons born to the union of the late Harry B. Patience and the late Elsie Miller Patience, was born at West Pittston, Pa. on August 27, 1906.

He was educated in the schools of West Pittston, graduating from West Pittston High School in 1924.

He received training in the art of coal carving from his father and pursued this career throughout his adult life. During his career as a creative artist, he achieved worldwide recognition for the excellence and imagination of his work. Magazines, radio, television, and other news media published or broadcasted many interviews and testimonials to his artistry. Several museums contain permanent exhibits of his work and many private collectors take pride in possessing his masterpieces.

He was united in marriage to the former Alice Patterson on September 16, 1948.

He was active in several fields of community and fraternal endeavors. He was a past president of Showcase Theater of Wilkes-Barre and served on the board of directors.

He was a past master of Golden Rule Lodge #15 Free and Accepted Masons and served as the District Deputy of the 9th Masonic District of the most Worshipful Prince Hall Grand Lodge, F and A.M. of Pennsylvania for ten years.

He was Worthy Patron of Mizpah Chapter #11 Order of Eastern Star and a former District Lecturer of the O.E.S. District of Deborah Grand Chapter.

He departed this life Wednesday June 7, 1972, at the age of 65 years, 9 months, and 10 days.

He leaves to mourn his passing a loving wife, Alice Patterson Patience; three children, Harry B. of Los Angeles, Calif., Mrs. Juanita Moss, Montclair, N. J., and Mrs. Etta Brown, Willingboro, N. J.; three brothers, Robert of Philadelphia, Wilmer and Harold, both of West Pittston; nine grandchildren; an aunt, Mrs. Lillian Cuff; several nieces and nephews; and a host of relatives and friends.

Appendix VII
Last Exhibit and Sale

Fig. 78. Cover of booklet for the Last Exhibit and Sale held at King's College, Wilkes-Barre, Pa., 1973

INTRODUCTION BY ALICE PATTERSON PATIENCE [116]

23 March 1973

To Friends of C. Edgar Patience:

Usually when an artist holds a one-man show, he is present to answer questions and to explain what he was expressing in a particular creation.

Since his show is being held after the death of the sculptor, the explanations in this brochure were written by his widow. She sincerely hopes that they do him and the work that he loved justice.

To understand a man's work, you must first understand the man. Edgar had two great loves in his life: people and coal.

Wherever he exhibited he was surrounded with people. He never tired of people: old people, young people, rich and famous people, poor and unknown people. He loved them all.

He completely enjoyed his work. To him, coal was the only medium from which to create the useful, the exciting, and the beautiful. He was happiest when surrounded by people who were admiring objects made from coal.

He was one of the rare artists who received some degree of fame during his lifetime. His works are in various parts of the world and wherever he went with his art, he received VIP treatment. His death is a great loss, not only to his family and friends, but also to the world since his highly skilled creative hands are now stilled.

For over forty years, Edgar created masterpieces out of anthracite coal. Since most of his work was commissioned, and not available for your inspection, his great versatility cannot be seen in this show. Only the pieces that remained after his death are on display for your enjoyment.

With great pride in the artist and with undying love for the husband and father, the family of the late C. Edgar Patience warmly welcomes you to this, his final art show.

DESCRIPTIONS OF ANTHRACITE SCULPTURES
FOR SALE
by
Alice Marie Patterson Patience

"AMALARICE"

This is a portrait of a woman with definite African features. The sculptor in naming her said that the name meant, "The Meek One." He quoted, "The meek shall inherit the earth." Hundreds of years of oppression and endurance are reflected in her eyes.

The artist's wife has been frequently asked if she were the model. The answer is no, unless subconsciously the artist modified the features. Her name is a combination of his wife's first and middle names (Alice Marie).

Fig. 79. *"Amalarice" at the Anthracite Heritage Museum in Scranton, Pa.*
(photo by Reba Burruss-Barnes 2004)

"ANTHRACITE"

The piece demonstrates stippled coal in its natural state. The surface is smoothed and engraved.

(Assistant District Attorney Ernest D. Preate, Jr. presented **"Anthracite"** to President Jimmy Carter at the White House in Washington, D.C., on 3 August 1977 when he signed one of the nation's first surface mining laws.)

"BLACK FRIDAY"

Most Christians refer to the day of the crucifixion of Jesus Christ as "Good Friday." C. Edgar Patience considered this a misnomer. To him it was the blackest day in Christian history, definitely not a day for rejoicing.

"COALTOWN—USA"

This is the most unusual item in the collection. The artist had worked on it at least twenty-five years. If he had lived twenty-five years longer, he would still be adding figures, homes, streets or machinery to this sculpture. It was never meant to be finished.

"Coaltown" was a "bus-man's holiday." When he wanted to think, relax, or just let his imagination run loose, he carved something else on this piece of coal.

The diorama represents a mining town of twenty-five to fifty years ago (in 2006, seventy-three years ago). *With infinite care as to detail, homes, streets, breakers, coal cars, shovels, miners, company stores, even street lights are depicted in this carving. It was a work of a lifetime and a labor of love*

("**Coaltown—USA,**" 12" wide x 12" long x 18" long is on permanent display at the Anthracite Heritage Museum in Scranton.)

ETCHINGS

Beautiful descriptive scenes can be etched by hand on coal. These delicate drawings were made by displacing minute particles of coal until the design the artist had in mind becomes apparent. When this is evident, the entire plaque is then highly polished.

Interestingly enough, the technique can be reversed. The plaque can be polished and then the artist removes chip by chip the unwanted coal until the design appears.

A few of the remaining etchings are the Pennsylvania Dutch **"Distelfink," "The Piper," "Midsummer's Night Dream,"** and a few others. Over the years most of these exquisite creations were sold.

"EZEKIEL'S WHEEL"

It is based on the Old Testament Prophet Ezekiel's vision of a wheel, "Way up in the middle of the air." In the Negro spiritual using this theme, "The big wheel turned by faith and the little wheel turned by the grace of God". Both wheels, as well as the stars and the Milky Way, are seen in the sculpture.

"GEOS"

"Geos" is an irregular shaped, highly polished coal sculpture. Some are very small. Others are quite large. Since they have many facets, they are radiant and reflect light. They required skill since only coal free from imperfections could be used. The shaping in order to get the greatest refraction of light also had to be considered.

"Geos" is an abbreviation for geological formation. Coal is a geological process formed by the earth's pressure on vegetation over a period of millions of years. Since the artist would use only the finest of coal to create these brilliant beauties, he named them after the process that produced the coal in the first place.

Fig. 80. *"Geos" property of Dorothy Walker Smith*
(courtesy of the owner, photo by Jim Collier 2006)

Fig. 81. *"Geos," property of Meyer Alprin of Scranton, Pa.*
(courtesy of the owner, photo by Warren Rowe 2005)

"HAIR"

This is a very interesting sculpture. Without a doubt, C. Edgar Patience was influenced by the current trend on the part of young males towards long hair. Long hair did not repulse him. He found it interesting as he did most things and tried faithfully to reproduce this sign of our time.

If someone told him that long hair on men was effeminate, he would laugh and reply, "Then this country was founded by a lot of effeminate men since all of the founding fathers had long hair."

He loved young people. "Hair" was his way of showing it. Although the face is highly polished, each strand of hair has been individually carved. He cared that much.

"LOVE"

Webster defines love as "a strong affection or liking for someone or something." The abstract sculpture entitled "Love" seems to be embracing the entire world. This was accomplished by the way the sculptor shaped the coal.

It is a highly polished free form set in a natural coal base. Many people have run their hands over it. They cannot seem to resist touching.

An inanimate object cannot respond to human sensitivity, but there is a quality in this sculpture that radiates love on first sight.

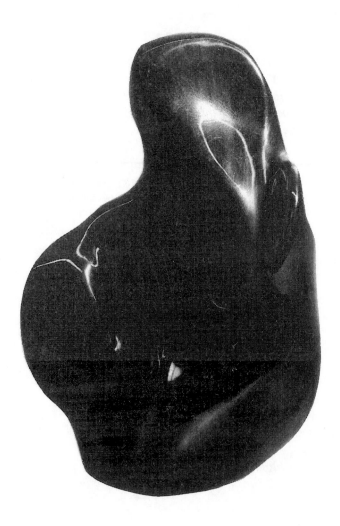

Fig. 82. *"Love," the property of Blue Cross of Northeastern Pennsylvania in*
Wilkes-Barre, Pa. (photo by Linda Paul 2005)

"KENNEDY"

The bust of John Fitzgerald Kennedy was the most highly
cherished by C. Edgar Patience and it was not to be sold until after his

death. Nine months of work went into the highly detailed work of several different textures, from his face, to his suit, to his tie, and his shirt.

"MAMA"

The sculptor took a new approach to a familiar theme. Fertility is represented by a female in this carving. Even among primitive peoples, the female figure is used to show that the source of life, as well as the sustenance of life rested with the female.

This concept is as old as time. Even the food that we eat is referred to as being a product of Mother Nature.

What is different in the portrayals? Unlike most paintings, the sculptor did not create a mother with a child at her breast. Instead, he carved a full breasted, stooping female with extended pelvis and massive buttocks. It is an unusual handling of a familiar theme.

"SERENDIPITY"

This figure represents many things to different people. Some say that is it a nun, others a figure of a woman. It is whatever you wish.

__Fig. 83.__ "Serendipity," the property of C. Edgar Patience's grand daughter, Brenda Moss Green

"SLAVE GIRL"

Among the outstanding pieces to be shown include **"Slave Girl,"** depicted primarily to show the origin of the black people in America. The beautiful young woman is pictured on a slave block with chains to represent her lack of freedom. The silver of the chains creates a striking contrast to the blackness of highly polished coal.

"STONE UPON STONE"

This is an assembled piece of three highly polished coal pieces. Each piece varies in size. After the pieces had been carved and polished, they were put together to create a modern art form. During the artist's lifetime, he made many variations on this theme. This art form fits any décor and was one of his most popular items although no two pieces were ever identical.

"UPWARD"

There are two sculptures entitled **"Upward."** The larger of the two is a highly polished curved piece of coal pointing skyward. The base is rough coal with four carved figures.

The smaller of the two has a natural coal base. There are no carved figures. Both sculptures were intended to show that man is always striving to move out of the earth-bound self to a higher plane where he might find release and ultimate peace. That only a few succeed in this quest, is vividly demonstrated by the expressions on the faces on the base of the larger sculpture.

MISCELLANEOUS ART ITEMS

C. Edgar Patience did a variety of art forms. Among those that remain are ashtrays, paperweights, miniatures, pen sets, and jewelry. He believed in creating for people of all income levels.

At one time he stated, "Never forget, Alice, that the person who has only $10.00 to spend may love beautiful things as much as the person who has $1,000.00"

This was his philosophy and he lived by it. Although it is not possible to list all of the small objects he left behind, they are on display. The most notable is the **"Egg,"** the only one he ever made for sale. Truly a work of art, it consumed a great deal of time and so he was willing to let it remain an original.

__Fig. 84.__ *"Eric's Egg" carved by C. Edgar Patience with his nine year-old grandson, Eric Douglas Moss in 1972 (property of Eric Moss, photo by Sabrina Rios)*

__Fig. 85.__ *"Elephant"*

According to C. Edgar Patience, *"No medium lends itself more to the creating of the simplified form of abstract art than does anthracite coal. Its rich velvety blackness when polished to perfection makes each sculpted piece unique and a delight to the eye.*

The sculpture called 'SHE' is an excellent representation of non-objective art. This work is many things to many people. Each person sees in this art form exactly what his own eye and experience dictate. Some see a seal—others a Madonna, and still others have seen simply the universal appearance of a woman.

The sculpture is all of these things and many more. It radiates warmth! It is eye appealing and when stroked it gives satisfaction to the sense of touch. It very simply says, 'Here I am. I will be whatever you want me to be. I was designed purely and simply to give pleasure.'

Art has no other real reason for existing except to give pleasure to the beholder. This 'SHE' does."

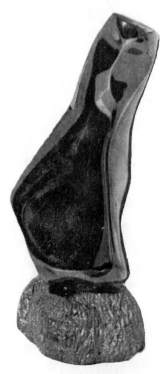

Fig. 86. "SHE," purchased by Lions International for Jorge Bird, President, Scranton, 21 May 1968

Appendix VIII
The Betty Patience Claiborne Collection

FIRST PUBLIC DISPLAY ON 26 AUGUST 2006
at the
THE ANTHRACITE HERITAGE MUSEUM
SCRANTON, PENNSYLVANIA

Abraham Lincoln bust-	10" tall, 5" wide
African Masks	male-6" x 3½"
	female-8" x 3½"
Ashtray	4" x 3½"
Bowl	6" in diameter
Candle holder pair	3¾" tall
Coal beads of a necklace, bracelet, and earrings	(117)
Coal Miner bust	3½" sitting on base;
	base-4" x 5"
Free form ashtray	12" x 12"
Free form figure	5½"; base 4"
	in diameter
Inkwell	4½" in diameter
Jewelry of coal and pyrite	
Jewelry of coal only	
Jewelry of pyrite ("Pa. diamonds") only	
Lion etching	7" x 4"
Pen holder	6½" x 4"
Shoe Horn	7" long
Vase (smaller)	3½" tall
Vase (taller)	10" tall, 3"
	in diameter

Fig. 87. Several pieces from the Betty Patience Claiborne Collection

Appendix IX
Correspondence

HOTEL CASEY

ABSOLUTELY FIREPROOF   GARAGE CONVENIENT

"Scranton's Leading Hotel"

SCRANTON 3, PENNA.

LACKAWANNA & ADAMS AVENUES

May 5 1948.

Harry B Patience's Sons.

Enclosing check for $11.00 owing charges on four Anthracite paper weights mailed to me at Chicago and one ordered today for D. H. HAIDER.

Thomas F. Lennon
Globe Coal Co.
332 S. Michigan Ave
Chicago, 4, Ill.

United Mine Workers of America

ADOLPH PACIFICO
PRESIDENT

DISTRICT No. 6

TEMPLE THEATRE BUILDING
PHONE 766

BELLAIRE, OHIO
August 25, 1952

Mr. Harry B. Patience & Sons
82 Loomis Street
Wilkes-Barre, Penns.

Attention: Mr. C. Edgar Patience

Re: Baseball Trophies

Dear Sir:

I acknowledge and thank you for your communication
of August 4, 1952, which is in reply to my letter to you of
July 28, 1952, regarding baseball trophies.

I regret, exceedingly, my delay in reply to yours of
August 4, 1952, which was due to my being absent from the
office.

I note, however, that you will be able to make an
ash-tray with the figure of a batsman in gold plate, mounted
in the place of the baseball on the tropy that I have at hand
for $7.50 each.

I further notice that the ash-tray will have a rough
cut well instead of the polished type and, the contour will
be somewhat irregular. I am of the opinion that an item of
this type will meet the approval of our Baseball League
Managers.

Accordingly, I am ordering twenty-five (25) of these
items at the rate of $7.50 each or a total of $187.50, plus
$21.60 for the trophy that I have in my possession or a
total of 209.10.

I shall deeply appreciate your preparing these items
and ship same as soon as possible. Upon receipt, I will forward you a check to the amount of $209.10, covering the order.

Kindly advise if this will meet with your approval.

With kindest personal regards, I am,

Sincerely yours,

Adolph Pacifico, President
District No. 6, U.M.W. of A.

U. M.   W. A.
District No. Six   Baseball League

ALVIN DOUGLAS, Vice President
Phone: Bell. 786 -- Adena 18

ANDREW POLLOCK, Secretary
Phone: Bpt. 596-J-2

ADOLPH PACIFICO, President
Phone: Bell. 786 – 845
TEMPLE THEATRE BUILDING
BELLAIRE, OHIO

June 19, 1953

Mr. C. Edgar Patience
82 Loomis St.
Wilkes Barre, Pa.

Dear Mr. Patience:

This will acknowledge receipt of your communication of
recent date in which you quote an estimate of $325 for the
large trophy and $250. for the smaller trophy.

In the event that your estimate is the maximum cost,
and you can guarantee that the trophies will arrive in
good condition, I think that we will order them made by
you. However, I would like assurance on this matter before
I make my final decision.

Further, as you know last year we ordered ashtrays from
you at a cost of $7.50 each. These were presented to each
Manager and officer of our League. We do not want to give
the same thing this year, and wold appreciate your sugges-
tions in this regard, cost not to exceed that of the ashtrays
and the baseball motif should be followed.

I would appreciate your earliest reply in order that I
may make my final decision as soon as possible, so that work
can begin on the trophies.

Sincerely yours,

Adolph Pacifico, President

ms

C. CRAWFORD HOLLIDGE
LTD.

Tremont at Temple Place
Boston

October 1, 1953

Harry B. Patience & Sons
82 Loomis Street
Wilkes Barre, Pennsylvania

Gentlemen:

We have an exhibit of your antharacite
jewelry in our window. The collection was loaned
to us by Miss Ruth McGowan of Newsome, Company.

We have a very fine specialty shop and
our customers have shown a great deal of interest
in your lovely jewelry.

Will you be kind enough to send us a
price list and also the style numbers of your
pieces, so that we may place an order with you.

Any further information you can send us
will be greatly appreciated.

Hoping to hear from you soon, we are,

Very truly yours,

C. CRAWFORD HOLLIDGE LTD.

E. M. Duffield

E.M. Duffield
Buyer of Jewelry

EMD:MP

Anthracite Information Bureau

1500 WALNUT STREET
SUITE 1414
PHILADELPHIA 2, PA.
PENNYPACKER 5-1834

November 24, 1953

Mr. Harry B. Patience
82 Lunnis Street
Wilkes-Barre, Pa.

Dear Harry:

Enclosed are nine (9) photos of the President. Please let me know whether you can develop a bust from these pictures. If so, we can then draw up a contract based on the price we had previously set.

Please take good care of these pictures, as they must be returned to Washington.

Sincerely yours,

George

GEORGE T. ADAMS

GTA:ub
Enc. 9

WESTERN UNION
TELEGRAPH

MAIN OFFICES & WAREHOUSES
LEOLA, PENNA.
PHONE LEOLA 6-2911

BRANCH OFFICES & WAREHOUSES
LANCASTER, PENNA.
138 SOUTH WATER ST.
PHONE LANCASTER 3141
RONKS, PENNA.
PHONE STRASBURG 3156
WITMER, PENNA.
PHONE LANCASTER 6412

January 6, 1954

Harry B. Patience's Sons
82 Loomis St.
Wilkes-Barre, Penna.

Dear Sir:

    Your wire received before Christmas was
mislaid and I came accross it today.

    I would like a necklace, bracelet and ear
ring set, for Mrs. Stauffer like the one you
made up for Miss America.

    Must you have neck and wrist sizes? If
not and you have a set ready please send it
to me registered mail.

    If you let me know the cost I will send
you a check in advance or as soon as I get
the set.

    Hope you can get the set to me soon.

          Yours very truly,

          H. M. Stauffer & Sons, Inc.

        per

CRS/dm

235 EAST 45TH STREET
NEW YORK 17, N. Y.
TELEPHONE: MURRAY HILL 2-5600
CABLE ADDRESS: BION, NEW YORK

June 19, 1957

Mr. George P. Benaglia
Kings College
Wilkes-Barre, Pa.

Dear Mr. Benaglia:

We should like to confirm the following information which has come to our attention:

"Kings College at Wilkes-Barre, Pa., has in its chapel, the only altar of coal in the world...It was made from a single block of Anthracite weighing about 4,200 pounds!"

Would you kindly verify this, and give us further information as to when and how this came about for a possible item in the BELIEVE IT OR NOT newspaper feature. We should also like to have a picture showing this altar.

The picture will be returned to you if you wish. Your kind cooperation will be greatly appreciated

Sincerely yours,
BELIEVE IT OR NOT!

Helen K. Kish
Office Manager

HKK:hkm

Courtesy of Dr. Margaret Corgan of King's College

The altar appeared in "Ripley's Believe it or Not" on Monday, 29 July 1975 in the *Wilkes-Barre Record.*

COURT OF COMMON PLEAS No. 1
JUDICIAL CHAMBERS
242 CITY HALL
PHILADELPHIA 7, PENNA.

EDWARD J. GRIFFITHS
JUDGE

October 19, 1960

Mr. Edgar Patience,
c/o Coal Novelties,
Loomis Street,
Wilkes Barre, Pa.

Dear Mr. Patience:

The Honorable William Lloyd Jones, of Pottsville, today presented me with a beautiful coal-electric clock which you made for him.

It is, indeed, a gorgeous piece of workmanship and one that I will prize all my life. I have placed it on my conference table where it will be seen by many, many persons each day.

As I look upon it from time to time I will not only think of my good friend, Bill Jones, but also of you, whose hands did such a magnificent piece of work.

Very sincerely yours,

EDWARD J. GRIFFITHS

EJG. b

PHOENIX CONTRACTING CO.

POST OFFICE BOX 433
POTTSVILLE, PA.

PHONE
XX*XXXXXX*X*XX*XXX
739-3311

July 7, 1966

Mr. Edgar Patience
82 Loomis Street
Wilkes-Barre, Pennsylvania

Dear Mr. Patience:

  John Jones would like you to make a $200.00 clock inscribed with the following name:

     THOMAS P. FOX, D.D.S.

  Please notify us when the clock is finished. Thank you,

     Very truly yours,

     PHOENIX CONTRACTING COMPANY

     MARY A. RYON

FILLING EVERY FOOT NEED

DR. PAUL J. McCABE
SURGEON CHIROPODIST
416 MINERS NATIONAL BANK BLDG.
WILKES-BARRE, PA.
—
VALLEY 4-8423

Dear Mr. Patieno:

May I add a personal compliment on the work that your doing on that "trunk" of coal. You certainly do have to have a lot of "Patience" in your occupation.

With all best wishes, I am,

Sincerely Yours,

Paul McCabe

"REAL FOOT COMFORT IS THE FOUNDATION OF THE COMFORT OF THE ENTIRE BODY"

Washington, D. C.

August 20, 1964

Mr. C. Edgar Patience
82 Loomis St.
Wilkes-Barre, Pa.

Dear Mr. Patience:

        264 Academy St., W-Barre,
I inquired of Miss Katherine Laidler/about some
coal novelties and she suggested I write to you.

    She stated you make up various pieces - some with
sulphur stone.

    Will you kindly advise me about the type of work
and the price; I may be able to secure some orders
for you.

    I formerly lived in W-Barre and feel that many people
might be interested in the coal articles if they knew
about them - especially, we who are from the Anthracite
Region and because some day we might not be able to
get them, and inasmuch as they are not mining coal to
the extent they did mine it. However, I shall
appreciate hearing from you and if you should have
a folder showing some of the designs, I should enjoy
receiving it. Especailly those with sulphur stone.

               Respectfully,

               Edith M. Andreas

1801 - 16th St., N. W.,
Apt. 108
Washington, D. C. 20009

WHO'S WHO IN AMERICA WA/DB (1B)
WITH WORLD NOTABLES

EDITORIAL OFFICES   CHICAGO, ILLINOIS 60611 U S A

1898 - Our Seventy-Second Year - 1970
August 26, 1970

Dear Mr. Patience:

On the basis of the standards outlined in the enclosed leaflet -
which standards were also described in our original letter - you
have been selected for listing in the next biennial edition of
WHO'S WHO IN AMERICA, Volume 37. Admission to WHO'S WHO assures
your place for all time in Who's Who in American History. It
also entitles you to nominate others for consideration for
inclusion by our Board of Editors.

As is the case with all Marquis listings, your name was selected in
an effort to meet serious reference demands, the only reason for a
biographical listing in WHO'S WHO or any other Marquis compilation.
With the aid of reference technicians our editors have developed
standards for inclusion, designed solely to assure as nearly as
possible coverage of all about whom reference inquiry may reasonably
be expected to occur, either because of achievements or positions,
or both. When a name has been selected as falling under these
standards, it must appear, or WHO'S WHO would be derelict in pro-
viding the coverage reference users expect it to supply.

Therefore, the editors are under standing instructions not to permit
under any circumstances the omission of a selected listing, and
these instructions are exactly as rigid as those prescribing that
their endeavor to meet reference needs may alone influence the
inclusion of names.

Naturally the editors desire, in the interest of mutually advantageous
accuracy, to include data personally supplied and checked by the
designated biographee. Accordingly, a duplicate biographical data
form, restricted to your use, is enclosed. It should be added, however,
that the editors will have no alternative, in the absence of your good
assistance, but to compile data from whatever sources are available.

It is our hope that this will not be necessary and that, appreciating
the need for meeting reference demands which WHO'S WHO serves, you
will now find it convenient to comply with our request by filling out
and returning the enclosed form at your earliest convenience.

Sincerely yours,

Gerald Burke

Gerald Burke

WA/DB
Three Enclosures

God Our Father · Christ Our Redeemer · Man Our Brother

Union African Methodist Episcopal Church
Easton, Pennsylvania

ISAAC N. PATTERSON, IV
Minister

June 19, 1971

Dear Bro Patience,

We thank you for your excellent craftmanship demonstrated in the desk set you designed for Bro. Bright.

Please excuse the delay in sending the check for the same.

Yours truly,

I. N. Patterson

President
Easton, N.A.A.C.P.

The Pittsburgh Press

PITTSBURGH, PA. 15230

April 5, 1972

Dear Mr. Patience,

Thank you for letting me borrow your material. I'm sure I didn't put it back in the same order I got it, but I think it's all there. I had copies of two pictures made, and if all goes well, the story should be in this Sunday's paper.

I hope you enjoy your stay in Pittsburgh.

Sincerely,

Ruth Heimbuecher

Ruth Heimbuecher
Travel Editor

COMMONWEALTH OF PENNSYLVANIA

PENNSYLVANIA HISTORICAL AND MUSEUM COMMISSION

BUREAU OF MUSEUMS

WILLIAM PENN MEMORIAL MUSEUM AND ARCHIVES BUILDING

BOX 1026

HARRISBURG, PENNSYLVANIA 17108

November 26, 1973

Mrs. C. Edgar Patience
82 Loomis Street
Wilkes-Barre, Pennsylvania   18702

Dear Mrs. Patience:

This letter will serve to introduce Mr. Michael Winey, Field Curator for the Bureau of Museums, who will pick up the two coal sculptures for delivery to Harrisburg: Coaltown and George Washington.

Mr. Winey will give you a Xerox copy of the Miscellaneous Order (No. 073430) which is used to process payment for this purchase. Since this is a "Confirmation Order," the original is used in the voucher for payment, hence the Xerox in this case. It does provide you with the data necessary to show that the purchase has been authorized.

At this moment I cannot tell you when payment will actually be made; it takes several weeks to go through all of the necessary offices, but you may be assured that things are in the works and well under way.

Very truly yours,

William N. Richards
Director, Bureau of Museums

WNR:kjb

C. EDGAR PATIENCE
Anthracite Coal Carving
82 LOOMIS STREET
WILKES-BARRE, PENNA.

PHONE VA 2-5526   November 29, 1973

Mr. F. W. Remington
Beaupland Road
Bear Creek, Pennsylvania

Dear Mr. Remington:

The sculpture that you purchased at the
Memorial Art Show of the late C. Edgar Patience
entitled, "Serenity" is an original. Edgar never
duplicated sculptures. Smaller works, not commissioned, such as ash trays, paperweights, bookends have been reproduced.

The sculptor's explanation of this creation
can be found on page eleven of the Memorial
booklet.

I hope that you and your family have many
years of enjoyment from this work of art.

Sincerely yours,

Alice

Mrs. C. Edgar Patience

AFRO-AMERICAN HISTORICAL AND CULTURAL MUSEUM

August 10, 1979

82 Loomis Street
Wilkes-Barre, PA 18702

Dear Mrs. Patience,

Thank you for your expression of Black pride. We have felt all along that Mr. Patience did not receive the proper acclaim and credit that he should have received for such creativity in a medium which was unique.

Within the next eight days we would like permission to review the pieces that are to be used in the planning of the catalog. You shall receive all credit due. Would it be possible for us to have a phone number where we may contact you for an appointment for such an interview? Please let me know when it would be convenient for such a meeting.

Last week, I sent a letter to Lloyd, my ex-roommate at Penn State inquiring as to your status. If you receive a message from him concerning the exhibition, please let him know I have heard from you.

As a point of interest, this is the first major exhibit of any state that is to commemerate the Black experience. It is to be as comprehensive as historically possible. We value your input and look forward to a further talk with you.

Sincerely,

Dr. Charles L. Blockson
Project Director

PENNSYLVANIA HISTORICAL AND MUSEUM COMMISSION

ANTHRACITE MUSEUM COMPLEX

Museum of Anthracite Mining
Pine & 17th Streets
Ashland, Pa. 17921
717-875-4708

Pennsylvania Anthracite Heritage Museum
R.D. 1, Bald Mountain Road
Scranton, Pa. 18504
717-963-4804

Eckley Miners' Village
R.R. 2, Box 236
Weatherly, Pa. 18255
717-636-2070

December 1, 1998

Mrs. Alice M. Patience
82 Loomis Street
Wilkes-Barre, PA 18702

Dear Mrs. Patience,

Please accept our thanks for your donation of the anthracite sculpture:
"Amalarice," by C. Edgar Patience. We are delighted to have the sculpture here in the
collections of the Anthracite Museum Complex. As we discussed, I have spoken with our
Director, Steven Ling, and we would like to have a reception with the exhibition of the
piece and invite members of your family when we have a return to nice weather in 1999.
Therefore, we will be asking you for addresses. Additionally, we will write the credit label
for the sculpture as: From: Mrs. Alice M. Patience and the descendants of C. Edgar
Patience.

Again, thank you so much for your continued kindness and generosity to the
Anthracite Museum Complex. We are grateful for your interest in the Museum and the
preservation of cultural heritage in northeastern Pennsylvania.

Sincerely,

Chester J. Kulesa, Curator
Anthracite Museum Complex

End Notes

1.Culm banks are man-made mountains of the debris of fine coal, coal dust, and dirt brought to the surface from coalmines.

2. Anthracosis, also called *pneumoconiosis* or "black lung disease," is caused by the long-term inhalation of coal dust.

3. Jim Kerstetter, "Fifty Who Mattered: Portrait of a People," *The Times Leader*, 25 April 1992, p. 10.

4. Joe Butkiewicz, "A Proud Legacy: Triumphs Throughout the Years," *Times Leader*, 27 April 1991, p. 8.

5. *Ibid.*

6. The Carboniferous Period is estimated to have occurred 299 to 359 million years ago.

7. Moh's scale classifies minerals based on relative hardness, determined by the ability of harder minerals to scratch softer ones. The scale includes the following minerals in order from softest to hardest: **1**. talc, **2**. gypsum, **3**. calcite, **4**. fluorite, **5**. apatite, **6.** orthoclase, **7**. quartz, **8**. topaz, **9**. corundum, **10**. diamond.

8. The author was quite surprised to see a familiar sight in Alaska: a culm bank located south of Fairbanks. The softer coal mined in Alaska is lignite, sub-bituminous, and bituminous.

9. C. Edgar Patience, "The Coal Industry."

10. *Ibid.*

11. *Ibid.*

12. Because of their coal mining experience and ability to speak English, the Welsh were among a privileged group of immigrants. "A Proud Legacy," p. 25.

13. Glen Hoffman, "Birth and Death of King Coal Displayed," *Citizen's Voice*, Wilkes-Barre, Pa., date unknown.

14. The sulfur found in coal can either be part of the carbonaceous material or of the minerals in the form of sulfates or sulfides. The noxious sulfur dioxide given off when coal burns has caused many deaths, particularly at night when people were asleep.

15. A conchoidal fracture is a smoothly curved break like that of broken glass or quartz.

16. *Ibid.*

17. Russell J. Charles, C.G., F.G.A., "The Challenge of Carving Coal Part II, An Ancient Lapidary Art," *Lapidary Journal*, April 1970, p. 138.

18. In 1662 King Charles of England granted to the people of Connecticut a strip of land from "sea to sea," including what is now the northern part of Pennsylvania. Later in 1681 he sold some of the same land to the people of Pennsylvania. In addition, Indians sold the same parcels of land to both the "Yankees" and "Pennamites" who engaged in several wars with the latter eventually becoming the victors. *A Proud Legacy*, p. 7.

19. A colliery is a workplace consisting of a coalmine plus all of the buildings and equipment connected with it.

20. A breaker is a tall colliery building with a peculiar shape seen nowhere else in the world. There chunks of coal are ground into useable sizes, such as the pea coal used for heating residences.

21. Coal company patches, such as Eckley's, were often just conglomerations of shanties for housing miners and their families.

22. At one time twenty-seven different European dialects were being spoken at the mines. (From research conducted at the Eckley Miner's Village located nine miles east of Hazelton, Pennsylvania.)

23. Jet is lignite, a very soft carbonaceous material.

24. "Coal Sculptor Practices an Ancient Art," source unknown, December 1969.

25. Alan L. Phillips, "Upstate Coal Carver Sculptures Bust of State Mines Secretary Charmbury," *Inquirer*, 14 December 1970.

26. *Ibid.*

27. Obituary, "Charles Cunningham Noted Coal Sculptor," source and date unknown.

28. John W. Cresbaugh, Jr., "Looking Them Over," *Montclair Times*, Montclair, New Jersey, 1971.

29. From a conversation between author and George Middleton, Department Chairperson of the Physical Education Department, Bloomfield High School, Bloomfield, New Jersey, April 2005.

30. *Times Leader* article, 16 June 2003.

31. Information from Frank Magdalinski.

32. Luther Dickey, *History of the 103rd Regiment: Pennsylvania Veteran Volunteer Infantry 1861-1865*, (Chicago, Illinois: L.S. Dickey), 1910, p. 84.

33. *Pittston Gazette*, 1928.

34. Juanita Patience Moss, *Created to Be Free*, Westminster, Md.: Willow Bend Books, 2001, p. 240.

35. "Report of The Inspectors of Mines of Pennsylvania," 31 December 1896, p. 100.

Conveyors carried coal up chutes for dumping into coal cars from which the anthracite was dumped yet again. This time it would be at the breakers where boys, some as young as seven or eight, huddled precariously over iron chutes ten hours a day, six days a week for the paltry sum of fifty cents a day. Their job was to separate the unusable slate and rock from good coal then ground into various sizes according to their usage.

36. Ted Fenstermacher, "Carver Shapes Anthracite: The Work of Patience," source unknown, 22 October 1967.

37. Obituary, "Death of Robert S. Miller: A Much Respected, Highly Esteemed Citizen of Hartley Township," *Mifflinburg Telegraph*, 2 April 1909. He was the town's first African American tax collector. Courtesy of Dr. Catherine Hastings, Susquehanna University, Selingsgrove, Pennsylvania.

38. No longer in existence, Bond Street was located between Linden Street and Wyoming Avenue on the north side of Luzerne Avenue.

39. Harriet Eldredge, "Black Jewelry is Beautiful: He Carves Coal Into Works of Art," *Bulletin*, 26 May 1971.

40. Sulfur pyrite is a sparkling crystalline matter that developed in the same area as the coal formation. What has been called "Pennsylvania Diamond" is now nearly impossible to find.

41. Close family friend Dorothy Walker Smith is a former resident of both Wilkes-Barre and Scranton.

42. From a conversation with Katherine Patience Kennedy in 2005.

43. *Ibid.*

44. Sally Teller Lottick, "C. Edgar Patience: Black Coal Sculptor," Our Valley Heritage, *Valley Panorama*, October 1987, p. 8.

45. *Ibid.*

46. *Ibid.*

47. The Northern Coal Field is a crescent-shaped geological area located in the counties of Luzerne and Lackawanna. The latter is the youngest of the sixty-seven Pennsylvania counties and prior to 1878 had been part of Luzerne County.

48. Alan Phillips, "Upstate Coal Carver Sculptures Bust of State Mines Secretary Charmbury," *Inquirer*, 14 December 1970.

49. Phillips.

50. C. Edgar Patience, "Coal Industry."

51. Phillips.

52. "Coal crackers" are notable sons and daughters of the anthracite coal region (Carbon, Columbia, Daughlin, Lackawanna, Luzerne, Northumberland, and Schuykill Counties).

53. "Hoover Carved Out of Anthracite," *The Ibaisaic*, 29 September 1934, p. 11.

54. Denise Widener, "C. Edgar Patience: Sculpting Identity Within a Regional and African-American Perspective, Part I," *Newsletter of the Pennsylvania Anthracite Heritage Museum and Iron Furnaces Associates*, Vol. 22, No. 1, January, February, March 2005, p. 4.

55. Alice Patterson Patience, *Bittersweet Memories of Home*, Wilkes-Barre, Pa.: Wilkes University Press, Vol. 1, p. 51.

56. Kay Dangerfield, "Palette: Vignettes of the Valley," source unknown, 11 February 1938.

57. "Here's Some Anthracite to See at World's Fair," a newspaper clipping, source unknown, 5 April 1939.

58. *Ibid.*

59. "King's College to Get Anthracite Altar," *Valley News*, 23 September 1954.

60. *Ibid.*

61. Rena Baldrica, "Anthracite Valley News," *The Wyoming Valley Observer*, 23-29 July 1972.

62. *Ibid.*

63. Dr. Margaret Corgan, memo from John B. Corgan, Jr. to Rev. George P. Benaglia, C.S.C., president of King's College in 1956.

64. Corgan, correspondence with author, 6 March 2006.

65. St. Peter's Lutheran Church, 1000 South Main Street, Hanover Township, Pa.

66. "Hall of Coal is Planned," a newspaper clipping, source unknown, Thursday, 15 December 1960.

67. Etheridge.

68. The monolith sits in a Smithsonian storage facility in Suitland, Maryland.

69. Patience, Vol. 1, p. 51.

70. "Guests to Receive Coal Souvenirs," a newspaper clipping, source and date unknown.

71. Lottick, p. 9.

72. Dr. Eugene Farley was the first president of Wilkes College.

73. Etheridge.

74. Christina Brinkley, "Flood Was Every Man's Champion," Fifty

Who Mattered: Portrait of a People, Profile '92, *Times Leader*, 25 April 1992, p. 38.

75. *Times Leader*, "Profile," 27 April 27 1991.

76. "But Calls It Not Strict Enough," a newspaper clipping, source unknown, 3 August 1977.

77. "Belmont Club Re-enacts 20-Year Gift to Flood," a newspaper article, source unknown, dated 1964.

78. Patience, Vol. 1, p. 49.

79. Lottick, p. 10.

80. *Ibid.*

81. *JET*, 23 October 1969; *EBONY*, March 1970.

82. Carolyn DuBose, "Coal-Black Art," *EBONY*, March 1970, p. 93.

83. *Ibid.*

84. Charles, p. 138.

85. *My Weekly Reader*, American Education Publications, Xerox Corp., Vol. 52, Issue 6, 21 October 1970, p.4.

86. Phillips.

87. "Bust Made By Patience Presented Charmbury," a newspaper clipping, source unknown, 10 October 1970.

88. Phillips.

89. "A Community Salute to Dr. H. Beecher Charmbury," program.

90. "C. Edgar Patience: Festival III Exhibitor's Coal Sculpture is Famous," *The Scrantonian*, 23 August 1970.

91. "Coal Sculptor Takes Part in Show," a newspaper clipping, source unknown, 29 May 1971.

92. "Patience's Art to be Shown in Philadelphia," a newspaper clipping, source unknown, dated 16 May 1972.

93. Etheridge.

94. *Ibid.*

95. *Mineral and Lapidary Society of Pittsburgh, Inc.*, Vol. XIX, 12 May 1972.

96. Minnie McClellan, "Late Edgar Patience Gains Sculpture Honor," *Sunday Independent*, Wilkes-Barre, Pa., 11 November 1973.

97. McClellan, from a newspaper clipping whose title and date are unknown to the author.

98. Mary Ann Kosik, "Century's Worst Flood: Susquehanna River Breaks All Flood Records Here," *The Observer*, 25 June-1 July 1972.

99. Baldrica.

100. Information from Frank Magdalinski in 2005.

101 "Patience Exhibit Opens at King's," newspaper clipping, source unknown, 12 March 1973.

102. *Ibid.*

103. Minnie McClellan, "Late Edgar Patience Gains Sculpture Honor."

104. Lottick, p. 10.

105. "But Calls It Not Strict Enough."

106. MacLellan.

107. *Of Color, Humanitias and Statehood: The Black Experience in Pennsylvania Over Three Centuries 1681-1981*, The Afro-American Historian and Cultural Museum, 1981, p. 123.

108. "King's College (Gently) Moves Coal Altar," *Citizen's Voice*, 18 August 1983.

109. Magdalinski.

110. Mary Therese Biebel, "Hard Coal Fueled His Dreams," *Times Leader*, 15 January 1998.

111. *EBONY*, p. 93.

112. Moss, p. 279. Monel metal is an alloy of nickel and copper.

113. *Who's Who in America* 1972, p. 2438.

114. *The Wyoming Valley Observer*, 25 June-1 July 1972.

115. Eulogy read at the funeral of Charles Edgar Patience on 10 June 1972.

116. Catalog from "King's College Final Exhibit and Sale," 12 March 1973.

117. Betty Patience Claiborne was wearing this anthracite coal jewelry when she was photographed with Pat Nixon in Washington, D.C. in October 1969.

__Fig. 88.__ "Flight" 3½"x 2¼"
(property of author)

Sources

BOOKS

Blockson, Charles. *Pennsylvania's Black History* (Philadelphia, Pa.: Portfolio Associates, Inc.), 1975.

Moss, Emerson I. *African Americans in the Wyoming Valley 1778-1990.* (Wilkes-Barre, Pa.: Wyoming Historical and Geological Society and the Wilkes University Press), 1992.

Moss, Juanita Patience. *Created to Be Free,* (Westminister, Md.: Willow Bend Books), 2001.

Of Color, Humanitias and Statehood: The Black Experience in Pennsylvania Over Three Centuries 1681-1981. (Philadelphia, Pa.: The Afro-American Historical and Cultural Museum), 1981.

Patience, Alice Patterson. *Bittersweet Memories of Home,* (Wilkes-Barre, Pa.: Wilkes University Press), 1999.

MAGAZINES

EBONY. Carolyn DuBose, "Coal-Black Art," March 1970.
JET. 23 October 1969.

NEWSPAPER ARTICLES

"3 ½ Ton Lump of Anthracite Will be Put on Display by Smithsonian Institution."

"A Chapel Fit For King's,' Matt Engel, *Shamrock Newspapers,* 5 January 2003.

"A Community Salute to Dr. H. Beecher Charmbury," Friday, 9 October 1970.

"Altar Holds Special Bond," Matt Engel, *Shamrock Newspapers,* 5 January 2003.

"Altar of Anthracite Dedicated at King's," *Times-Leader,* 22 October 1956.

Anthracite Valley News, Rena Baldrica, *The Wyoming Valley Observer,* 23-29 July 1972.

"Belmont Club Re-enacts 20-Year Gift to Flood."

"Birth and Death of King Coal Displayed," Glen Hoffman, *Citizen's Voice.*

"Bishop McCormick Blesses Chapel New Campus Ministry Ceneter," *The Catholic Light,* 15 March 1984.

"Black Jewelry is Beautiful: He Carves Coal into Works of Art," Harriet Eldridge, *Bulletin.*

"Bust Made by Patience Presented to Charmbury."

"But Calls It Not Strict Enough."

"Carver Shapes Anthracite, The Work of Patience," Ted Fenstermacher, 22 October 1967.

"C. Edgar Patience: Black Coal Sculptor, Sally Teller Lottick, *Our Valley Heritage.*

"C. Edgar Patience Festival III Exhibitor's Coal Sculpture is Famous."

"C. Edgar Patience, 65, Coal Sculptor, Dies."

"C. Edgar Patience Dies; Sculptor Stricken on Tour."

"Charles Cunningham Noted Coal Sculptor."

"Charmbury in Coal."

"City Man Exhibits Coal Sculpture at Washington National Crafts Show," Minnie B MacLellan, *Sunday Independent,* 8 February 1970.

"Coal Altar Decked for Yule."

"Coal Sculptor at Montreal Exposition," 14 August 1971.

"Coal Sculptor Practices and Ancient Art," December 1969.

"Coal Sculptor Shows Techniques at Fine Arts Fiesta."

"Coal Sculptor Takes Part in Show," 29 May 1971.

"Coaltown—USA and Washington Bust Can Be Seen at Anthracite Museum," 17 February 1997.

"College Chapel Has Anthracite Altar," *The Boston Traveler,* January 1957.

"College Chapel Has Anthracite Altar," *The Ocean Press,* Friday, 19 April 1957.

"Dallas Rotary Club to Hold September Fair," 7 August 1956.

"Four-Ton Anthracite Altar Moved To New Chapel at King's College," *Sunday Independent,* Wilkes-Barre, Pa. 4 July 1971.

"Guests to Receive Coal Souvenirs."

"Hall of Coal Planned," 15 December 1960.

"Hard Coal Fueled His Dreams," For Kids Today, Mary Therese Biebel, *Times Leader,* Thursday, 15 January 1998.

"Here's Some Anthracite to See at World's Fair," 5 April 1939.

"King's College Dedicated New Chapel," *Times Leader*, 25, February 1984.

"King's College (Gently) Moves Coal Altar," *Citizen's Voice*, Wilkes-Barre, Pa., Thursday, 18 August 1983.

"King's College to Get Anthracite Altar," *Valley News*, 23 September 1954.

"King's Has Anthracite Altar, *"Wilkes-Barre Record*, 22 October 1956.

"King's Opens Doors of New Chapel, Ministry Center," *Times Leader*, 20 February 1984.

"Late Edgar Patience Gains Sculpture Honor," Minnie MacLellan, *Sunday Independent*, Wilkes-Barre, Pa., 11 November 1973.

"Local Artist Puts Energy Into Coal Creations," *Times Leader*, Wilkes-Barre, Pa., 16 June 2003.

"Local Coal Carver Called 'Most Unusual Sculptor.'"

"Local Native Was Internationally Known Artist," Jack Smiles, *Sunday Dispatch*, 5 February 2006.

"Magazine Cites Work of Local Sculptor."

"Mailbag Bulletins: King's Has Coal Altar," Hal Boyle, New York, 14 May circa 1956.

"Memorial Exhibit to Show Work of the Late C. Edgar Patience," Minnie MacLellan, *Sunday Independent*, Wilkes-Barre, Pa., 25 February 1973.

"Palette: Vignettes of the Valley," Kay Dangerfield, 11 February 1938.

"Palmerton Hospital Festival is Reported A Tremendous Success."

"Patience Exhibit Opens at King's," 12 March 1973.

"Patience's Art to Be Shown in Philadelphia," Tuesday, 16 May 1972.

"Ripley's Believe It or Not," *Wilkes-Barre Record*, 29 July 1957.

"Skilled Coal Carver Remains a Mystery to Many Area People," *Citizens Voice*, Wilkes-Barre, Pa."

"Striking Chancel Area of New Lutheran Church."

"Strange As It Seems," Elsie Hix, *Pittsburgh Press, Reading Eagle-Times, Allentown Chronicle*, 17 March 1957.

"The Story of C. Edgar Patience, Internationally Known Artist."

"Trophy for Anthracite Golf Meet," 27 September 1951.

"'Unusual' Brilliance," Tom Long, *Citizen's Voice,* 12 February 2006.

"Upstate Coal Carver Sculptures Bust of State Mines Secretary Charmbury," Alan L. Phillips, *Inquirer,* 14 December 1970.

OTHER PUBLICATIONS

"African American Laborers in Luzerne and Lackawanna Counties," a paper by Eric Ledell Smith, Associate Historian, Pennsylvania Historical and Museum Commission for the *Tenth Annual Conference on the History of Northeast Pennsylvania, the last 100 years,* Luzerne County Community College, Nanticoke, Pa., 9 October 1998.

Anne Paye, R.S.M., "Wilkes-Barre Afro-Americans' Stories Bittersweet," *The Searcher,* Newsletter of the Genealogical Research Society of Northeastern Pennsylvania, Vol. 5, No. 4, Winter 2000.

A Proud Legacy: Triumphs Through the Years, Profile '91, T*imes Leader,* 27 April 1991.

Alice Patterson Patience, "Black is Indeed Beautiful."

Bradford Willard, *Pennsylvania Geology Summarized,* Educational Series No. 4, 1962.

Christine Patterson, *The Black Experience in Wyoming Valley,* (Wilkes-Barre, Pa.: Wilkes University Press), 1987.

Denise Widner, "C. Edgar Patience: Sculpting Identity Within a Regional and African-American Perspective," Parts I and II, *The Miner's Lamp;* April, May, June 2005.

"Fifty Who Mattered: Portrait of a People, Profile '92," A *Times Leader* Special.

Mineral and Lapidary Society of Pittsburgh Inc., Vol. XIX, "Wilkes-Barre Coal Sculptor Lures Visitors," 19 May 1972.

My Weekly Reader, Vol. 52, Issue 6, 21 October 1970.

Our Valley Guide, Valley Panorama, October 1987.

Showcase Theatre Playbill, 1972.

Russell J. Charles, C.G., F.G.A., "The Challenge of Carving Coal Parts 1 and II, An Ancient Lapidary Art," *Lapidary Journal*, March 1970.

The Mining and Preparation of D&H Anthracite, The Hudson Coal Company, Scranton, Pa., 1944.

William E. Edmunds and Edwin F. Koope, *Coal in Pennsylvania*, Educational Series No. 7, 1968.

***Fig. 89**. Monolith at Anthracite Heritage Museum in Scranton, Pa.
(photo by Reba Burruss-Barnes)*

Fig. 90. C. Edgar Patience working in "The Shop"
West Pittston, Pa. circa 1950
(courtesy of Roy Kylander)

Index

PHONE 822-5526

C. EDGAR PATIENCE

ANTHRACITE COAL CARVING

82 LOOMIS STREET   WILKES-BARRE, PA. 18702

Fig. 91. Business card of C. Edgar Patience

OTHER BOOKS BY JUANITA PATIENCE MOSS

CREATED TO BE FREE
ISBN: I-58549-704-5

This historical novel is based on the life of an 18 year-old runaway slave boy who joined the 103rd Pennsylvania Regiment when it was garrisoned in Plymouth, N.C. The reason for writing this book was because several historians told the author that there had been no black soldiers in white regiments during the Civil War. Juanita Patience Moss, however, knew differently because her great grandfather had been one.

Her research to discover if there had been other such men led to her writing about her ancestor's 83 year life journey from the sweet potato fields of North Carolina to the anthracite coal fields of northeastern Pennsylvania. Escaping from Chowan County, the slave boy Toby, became the free man Crowder Pacien (Patience.)

Through the letters of a fictitious "Plymouth Pilgrim," the story of the Battle of Plymouth is told. A particularly poignant passage deals with what happened to two North Carolina "Buffaloes" who were brothers.

Readers interested in the coal mining industry will want to read about the plight of seven and eight year-olds who were "breaker boys" working ten hour days, six days a week. Seemingly, the coal mining industry had created another kind of slave.

Created to Be Free is about one American family, in some ways very different from others, but in many other ways paralleling them. It is a universal story of tenacity and of survival. Therefore, this book has something for everyone, regardless of ethnicity.

BATTLE OF PLYMOUTH, N.C., APRIL 17-20, 1864: THE LAST CONFEDERATE VICTORY

ISBN- I-58549-852-1

This nonfiction book tells of the role played by a small southern inland town during the Civil War. Plymouth, N. C. was a vital Confederate port on the Roanoke River and so the Union needed to blockade the area.

The second largest battle in North Carolina occurred at Plymouth. Intense drama took place during four days filled with surprise, fate, intrigue, bravery, ingenuity, hope, daring, dedication, gallantry, disappointment, culminating in victory for the South and defeat for the North.

Called the "most daring mission during the Civil War," William Cushing six months after the battle was able to destroy the *CSS Albemarle*, the ironclad built in a cornfield. The History Channel in May of 2005 aired a documentary concerning how the Yankees were able re-occupy Plymouth until the end of the war in 1865.

Little has been written about the Battle of Plymouth and so this interesting and informative book will be of value to Civil War buffs, as well as students of American History. Even 141 years after the acrimonious war ended, new facts are still being uncovered.

FORGOTTEN BLACK SOLDIERS IN WHITE REGIMENTS DURING THE CIVIL WAR.

ISBN 0-7884-3332-8

History books include no information concerning the fact that black soldiers served in white regiments during the Civil War. Only members of the United States Colored Troops (USCT) are recorded.

Since Crowder Pacien (Patience), great grandfather of Juanita Patience Moss, served in the 103rd Pennsylvania Volunteers, a white regiment, she was aware of at least one black soldier in one white regiment. She wanted to find out if there had been more, and there were.

Because of residing in Alexandria, Virginia, she was able to delve into military records housed at the National Archive and the Library of Congress in Washington, D.C. Subsequently, she has published the names of more than 1000 blacks serving in white regiments. These names could fill an additional regiment of black soldiers whose memories need to be honored, too.

The list presented here is only an introduction because there are many names yet to be retrieved from the National Archives. This list may validate a family's oral history that says an ancestor had served in the Civil War, but his name is not on the monument in Washington or in the National Parks Database. It may even uncover additional roles played by black soldiers heretofore unknown to historians simply because they do not know black soldiers in white regiments existed.

JUANITA PATIENCE MOSS

Juanita Patience Moss, the daughter of the late Charles Edgar and Cora Johnson Patience, is a former New Jersey high school biology teacher. A product of the West Pittston Public School system, she attended Bennett College, Greensboro, N.C.; received a BS degree from Wilkes College, Wilkes-Barre, Pennsylvania; and a MA degree from Fairleigh Dickinson University, Rutherford, New Jersey.

After her retirement in 1992 from Bloomfield High School, Bloomfield, New Jersey, she developed an interest in genealogy and decided to write a historical novel. *Created to Be Free* is based on the life of her great grandfather, Crowder Patience, a runaway slave who enlisted at the age of eighteen in the 103rd Pennsylvania Volunteer Regiment garrisoned in Plymouth, North Carolina, during the Civil War.

The nonfiction books, *Battle of Plymouth, N.C., April 17-20, 1864:The Last Confederate Victory,* and *Forgotten Black Soldiers in White Regiments During the Civil War*, followed due to the value of her research. She also has edited two small volumes, *Bittersweet Memories of Home*, the memoirs of her blind stepmother, Alice Patterson Patience.